KNIT
LOCAL

sixth&spring books
New York, NY

TANIS GRAY

KNIT LOCAL

Celebrating America's Homegrown Yarns

sixth&spring books

Library of Congress
Cataloging-in-Publication Data

Gray, Tanis.
   Knit local : celebrating America's
homegrown yarns / Tanis Gray.
      p. cm.
   ISBN 978-1-936096-18-3 (pbk.)
   1. Knitting--United States. 2.
Knitting--Patterns. 3. Yarn--
United States. I. Title.
   TT819.U6G73 2011
   746.432--dc23

                    2011017990

Manufactured in China

1 3 5 7 9 10 8 6 4 2

First Edition

Acknowledgments

For Roger, my North Star, my guiding light, thank you for turning a
blind eye to the late-night writing and knitting sessions, the piles of yarn,
the sticky notes everywhere, the lack of use of the kitchen table for months
while it became my work space, and for being my tech support.
You're a good sport and an amazing husband.

To Mom and Dad, who put knitting needles in my hands, a good head on
my shoulders and sent me to art school, thank you for the constant
encouragement and support.

To Callum, our beautiful son born during the making of this book.
You make every day a joy.

To the intrepid staff at SoHo Publishing, my former family and
amazing coworkers, Trisha Malcolm, David Joinnides, Wendy Williams,
the very helpful Michelle Bredeson, Alexandra Joinnides, Sarah Liebowitz,
Loretta Dachman, Joe Vior and the talented Diane Lamphron, you made
this book a pleasure to work on.

To the lovely and charismatic Erica Smith, I salute you and
thank you for the care you gave this book.

To Uli Monch, Pat Hartse and Stephanie Mrse, a gracious thanks.

To the incredibly skilled and crafty knitters who contributed
designs to this book, I feel honored to be in such company and
I commend you on your creativity.

Finally, to all the wonderful and generous yarn companies who supplied
fiber and knowledge for this book, thank you for putting your faith in me,
filling my head with ideas and being so kind.

Managing Editor
WENDY WILLIAMS

Senior Editor
MICHELLE BREDESON

Art Director
DIANE LAMPHRON

Book Editor
ERICA SMITH

Instructions Editor
PAT HARSTE

Instructions Proofreader
STEPHANIE MRSE

Editorial Assistant
ALEXANDRA JOINNIDES

Technical Illustrations
LORETTA DACHMAN
ULI MONCH

Page Layout
MICHELLE HENNING

Principal Photography
SCOTT JONES

Additional Photography
MARCUS TULLIS
ROSE CALLAHAN

Fashion and Prop Stylist
SARAH LIEBOWITZ

Hair and Makeup
ELENA LYAKIR

Vice President, Publisher
TRISHA MALCOLM

Creative Director
JOE VIOR

Production Manager
DAVID JOINNIDES

President
ART JOINNIDES

Contents

KNIT LOCAL

■ INTRODUCTION

Why Knit Local?

What are the benefits to buying local? These days we find ourselves inundated with commercials and ads telling us to buy local, that local is better and that we should boycott overseas products. We are told to buy local without being told the benefits, and the benefits are what make it worthwhile.

Local is a broad term, one with varied definitions. It can mean buying honey from your neighbor's beehives or buying something across the continent. By keeping your business in the same country, or even in your neighborhood, studies have shown that more of that money returns back to the community, strengthening the economy and providing more local jobs. By buying local you are in turn supporting yourself.

Another major benefit to purchasing local goods is the environmental impact. Local businesses tend to make more local purchases, which require lower or little transportation costs. Being able to send items on a truck or even a bicycle means no international shipping, less oil and gasoline, reduced fumes, less pollution and faster turnaround

time. It gives the business owners more time to spend developing their product and getting to know their customers than waiting for freight and contributing to climate change and resource consumption.

When purchasing yarn in a yarn shop, not every knitter thinks about where it came from. Few wonder about the sheep, alpaca or yak it was taken from, the farm they grew up on or who dyed it for them. They don't consider the fiber being processed or what it took to get the yarn from sheep to skein, so to speak. Buying local doesn't just stop at apples from the farmer's market or cotton T-shirts—it can be found in the most surprising places!

Many of the yarn companies featured in this book have seen their product through its entire lifespan. They were there when the animal was born, raised and bred it, sheared it, processed the fiber, dyed it, spun it, put labels on it and got it to your local yarn shop. In today's society we've lost track of the journey our yarn makes. Living in a city myself, the only time I see animals is when I visit the National Zoo. Being a farmer is one of the most difficult jobs out there, with a 24/7, never-ending shift. To not only raise the animals but make the fleeces into beautiful yarn is the ultimate example of sustainability.

What is sustainability? It's a term that's thrown around a lot

today, part of the "greenwashing movement" to make large businesses more appealing to the average consumer. A truly sustainable product is one that follows the triple bottom line paradigm: balancing social, environmental and economic factors. How does this play into yarn and the criteria of this book?

When I began doing research for this book, I was pleasantly surprised at the number of companies found here in the United States that followed the yarn-making process from sheep to skein. The fibers in this book were not taken from across the globe and imported here. The fleeces come from the U.S., are made into fiber, dyed and milled here and shipped out all over the world. Talking to the owners about their shearing, dyeing and milling processes was not only interesting but also inspiring. The yarns in this book are truly local products.

Many of the companies found in this book hold their animals and the environment paramount. They think about run-off water from their dye process and how they can recycle that water on their land. Do they use natural or chemical dyes? What damage do their animal's feet do to the pastures? Can they use slower shipping to drive cost down for the consumer? How can they keep their animals happy and healthy? How will the knitter feel working with their end product? It is indeed a circle-of-life process on the farm whether you're raising the animals yourself or bringing fleece in from local farmers.

Knitting and crocheting are social activities. Crafting has brought people together for centuries, and with the combination of new technology and old-school techniques, we not only keep things local by meeting with our neighborhood knitting group but are able reach out to those on the other side of the world working on the same project. Local and global are merging together at a lightning-quick pace in the crafting community.

Next time your find yourself in your local yarn shop or at your farmer's market, talk to someone about where the fiber in your hands is from. How was it made? Where was it milled? What kind of dye process was used? The more you understand about your fiber and where it came from, the more informed you will be and the more you'll appreciate the process. There's so much more to yarn than going to your LYS and purchasing what's new and pretty. The yarn in your hands has a life cycle just like we do, and it's a fantastic journey.

Happy knitting!

Tanis

CHAPTER 1

Northeast

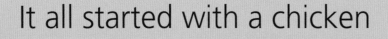

■ MOREHOUSE FARM MERINO

It all started with a chicken

Company Stats

COMPANY STARTED
1983

PROPRIETORS
Margrit Lohrer and
Albrecht Pichler

LOCATION
Red Hook, New York

YARNS
Twelve types, all made in the
United States

BUSINESS PHILOSOPHY

*To run a profitable
textile enterprise with a
product that's grown
and manufactured in
the United States.*

WEBSITE
morehousefarm.com

Morehouse Farm Merino began 30 years ago with a chicken. Margrit Lohrer and Albrecht Pichler lived and worked in New York City and owned a country house a hundred miles north. On her way to work one day, Lohrer caught a stray rooster near a park favored by voodoo practitioners for their rites.

The chicken, having escaped its fate as religious sacrifice, started a new life in the country where a few weeks later it was joined by a dozen hens from a neighbor's flock. Lohrer and Pichler started to seriously think about farming and what animal to choose for an agricultural enterprise that would warrant a career switch and a permanent move to the country.

For Lohrer, an avid knitter, raising merino sheep was an easy choice. In 1983, the winning flock of sheep at the National Merino Show made the trip from Pennsylvania to Red Hook, New York. The small starting flock grew rapidly into over 600 sheep. To Lohrer's delight, the merino wool shorn off the sheep spun into supersoft merino knitting yarn. Morehouse Farm Merino was born!

Lohrer's training as a graphic designer was put to new use in creating knitted garments and stuffed animals. Her animal-inspired scarf, mitten and hat designs garnered Morehouse Farm an enthusiastic following the world over from knitters of all ages. Their easy-to-understand knitting patterns, written without abbreviations or customary knitting symbols, have made it possible for knitters of all skill levels to enjoy creating their own critters.

Morehouse has since grown into a company that relies on many merino breeders from across the country to supply their ever-growing need for quality merino wool. Their own flock of sheep at the farm has dwindled to a hundred, and the former sheep barns have almost all been converted to wool storage warehouses.

A truly homegrown business, Morehouse Farm Merino wool is not only grown in America, but also processed entirely in the United States—from scouring (washing) the raw wool, to carding, spinning and dyeing the finished skeins.

1. Albrecht Pichler at feeding time
2. Ready for his close-up!
3. Merino sheep before shearing
4. The flock in snow

■ MOREHOUSE FARM MERINO

Bipartisan Pillows

■■■□

FINISHED MEASUREMENTS
14" x 14"/35.5cm x 35.5cm
(excluding trim)

MATERIALS
■ 5 2oz/57g hanks (each approx
140yd/128m) of Morehouse Farm
Merino *Worsted* (merino wool) in
soft white (A) **(4)**
■ 3 hanks in royal (B)
■ 1 hank in cardinal (C)
■ One pair size 8 (5mm) needles
or size to obtain gauge
■ Stitch markers
■ Nineteen 1⅜"/35mm white star
buttons
■ Three 14" x 14"/35.5cm x
35.5cm pillow forms

GAUGE
14 sts and 20 rows to
4"/10cm over St st using size 8
(5mm) needles.
Take time to check gauge.

Being a resident of Washington,
DC, and living on Capitol Hill, I
see that politics are on everyone's
mind. With major decisions for
the country being made literally
outside my front door, I wanted
to represent the vibe of my new
city in a nonpartisan way with
needles and yarn.

DONKEY PILLOW (make 2)
With A, cast on 60 sts. Work in
garter st for 10 rows.
Next row (RS) K5, pm, k50, pm, k5.
Next row K5, sl marker, p50, sl
marker, k5. Keeping first and last 5
sts in garter st and center 50 sts in
St st, work even until piece measures 13"/33cm from beg, end with
a WS row. Work in garter st for 10
rows. Bind off knitwise.

LACE TRIM
With B, cast on 5 sts.
Row 1 (RS) K3, yo twice, k2—7 sts.
Row 2 K3, p1, k3.
Rows 3 and 4 Knit.
Row 5 K3, yo twice, k2tog, yo
twice, k2—10 sts.
Row 6 K3, p1, k2, p1, k3.
Row 7 Knit.
Row 8 Bind off first 5 sts, k4—5 sts.
Rep rows 1–8 forty-three times
more. Bind off knitwise.

FINISHING
To center chart for duplicate stitch
embroidery on front, count 12 St
sts from RH garter st border (mark
with a pin), count 7 St sts from LH
border (mark with a pin), then
count 12 St st rows up from top of
bottom border (mark with a pin).
Using tapestry needle, embroider
duplicate stitches (see page 149)
using B and C foll chart. Block piece
lightly. Referring to photo, sew on
three buttons using A. With WS
facing, sew pieces together,
inserting pillow form before sewing
closed. Sew ends of trim tog.
Whipstitch trim to outer edge of
pillow, positioning seam at lower
RH corner.

ELEPHANT PILLOW
Work as for donkey pillow. Work
lace trim using C.

FINISHING
To center chart for duplicate stitch
embroidery on front, count 11 St
sts from RH garter st border (mark
with a pin), count 9 St sts from LH
border (mark with a pin), then
count 12 St st rows up from top of
bottom border (mark with a pin).
Using tapestry needle, embroider
duplicate stitches (see page 149)
using B and C foll chart.
Cont as for donkey pillow.

NORTHEAST

ORIGINAL 13 COLONIES PILLOW

Work as for donkey pillow using B.
Work lace trim using A.

FINISHING

Referring to photo, sew on thirteen
buttons in a circle using A.
Assemble pillow and sew on trim
as for donkey pillow. ●

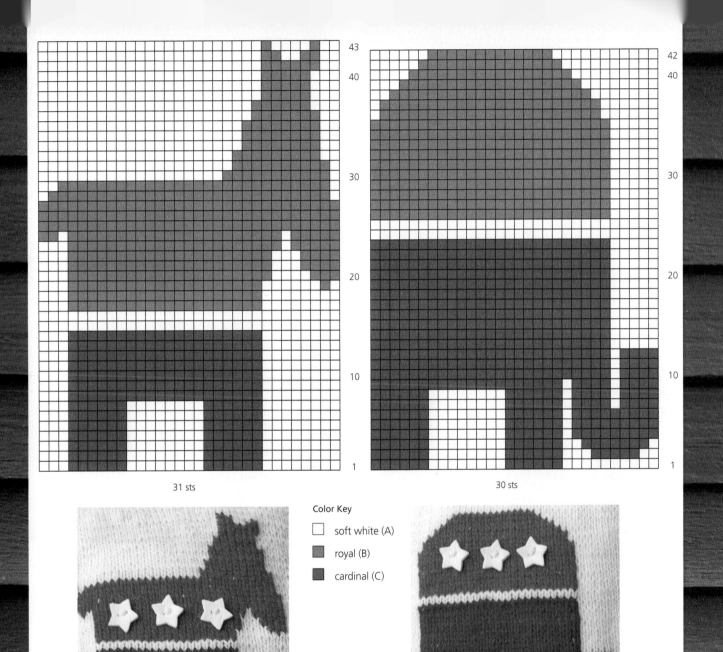

43
40
30
20
10
1

31 sts

42
40
30
20
10
1

30 sts

Color Key

☐ soft white (A)

■ royal (B)

■ cardinal (C)

■ FARMHOUSE YARNS

A one-woman yarn business

Company Stats

COMPANY STARTED
2001

PROPRIETOR
Carol Martin

LOCATION
East Haddam, Connecticut

YARNS
Twelve types, all made in
the United States

BUSINESS PHILOSOPHY
*To stick to basic
principles: take care,
have fun and keep it
local as much as
possible.*

WEBSITE
farmhouseyarns.com

Farmhouse Yarns was truly a hobby-turned-career for owner Carol Martin, who was working in industrial sales when she began to explore opportunities in the yarn business.

Through the years Martin has developed a business philosophy of keeping the business as American as possible. That means purchasing American fibers with wool coming directly from American farmers, many with small family farms with twenty or fewer sheep, including Martin's own flock; creating the yarn locally; and supporting the industry by offering creative opportunities to others new to the business. Martin does this by getting to know her customers on a first-name basis and answering the phone herself one hundred percent of the time. The positive relationships she has built with customers, farmers, mills, suppliers and fiber-loving friends is what makes running the business worthwhile to her.

Farmhouse Yarns are hand-dyed so each skein is a unique and beautiful work of art. There is no such thing as dye lot. Variegations within each skein depend on the location of each skein of yarn in the dye pot. Typically, skeins at the bottom of the pot are deep and rich in color, and skeins at the top of the pot have more subtle shades of color. It is recommended that when you are knitting with this yarn, you alternate skeins by working a few rows from one skein, then working a few more with another skein throughout your work so that the variegation is evenly distributed.

It is extremely important to Martin to be directly involved in the entire process from beginning to end. She is known not only for the vibrant colors of her yarns, but for being an all-in-one yarn provider.

There are not many yarn companies in which the owner is also the sheep farmer, shearer, lambing midwife, color creator, yarn producer and dyer, customer service person, order packer, pattern designer and wool broker all at the same time. This is what makes Farmhouse Yarns unique in the industry and creates a great environment for doing business: When a customer has a question, Martin can give him or her the best personal attention because she made the yarn and packed the order herself.

1. Yarn drying in the sun

2. Another new face

3. Carol Martin's daughter, Mary, feeding a newborn lamb

■ FARMHOUSE YARNS

Cabled Car Coat

■■■■

SIZES
Instructions are written for Small. Changes for Medium, Large and X-Large are in parentheses.

FINISHED MEASUREMENTS
BUST (Closed) 34 (38, 42, 46)"/86.5 (96.5, 106.5, 117)cm
LENGTH 30½ (31, 31½, 32)"/77.5 (78.5, 80, 81)cm
UPPER ARM 12½ (13½, 14½, 15½)"/31.5 (34, 37, 39.5)cm

MATERIALS
■ 10 (12,13,14) 4oz/113g hanks (each approx 200yd/183m) of Farmhouse Yarns *Andy's Merino* (merino wool) in chili pepper ④
■ One pair each sizes 8 and 9 (5 and 5.5mm) needles *or size to obtain gauge*
■ Size 8 (5mm) circular needle, 36"/91cm long
■ Cable needle (cn)
■ Size G-6 (4mm) crochet hook
■ Stitch markers
■ Five 2"/50mm toggles
■ Five 1"/25mm metal snaps
■ Six ⅝"/16mm flat buttons

GAUGE
21 sts and 22 rows to 4"/10cm over bamboo st using larger needles. *Take time to check gauge.*

When Sauniell Connally was a teen, she fell in love with an expensive hooded car coat, and with her mother's help, sewed her own. She cherished the coat and the idea that it was specifically made for driving, a distinctly American concept. Those memories inspired her to create an updated sweater version that can worn whether you are walking or driving, in the city or the country.

STITCH GLOSSARY
6-st RC Sl next 3 sts to cn and hold to *back*, k3, k3 from cn.
6-st LC Sl next 3 sts to cn and hold to *front*, k3, k3 from cn.

BAMBOO STITCH
(over a multiple of 2 sts)
Row 1 (RS) K1, *yo, k2, pass yo over 2 sts on RH needle; rep from *, end k1.
Row 2 Purl.
Rep rows 1 and 2 for bamboo st.

RIB PATTERN
(over a multiple of 5 sts)
Row 1 (RS) K1, *k3, p2; rep from *, end k4.
Row 2 P1, *p3, k2; rep from *, end p4.
Rep rows 1 and 2 for rib pat.

BACK
With smaller needles, cast on 110 (120, 130, 140) sts. Work in rib pat

for 3"/7.5cm, end with a RS row. Change to larger needles. Purl next row. Cont in bamboo st and work even for 2"/5cm, end with a WS row.

SIDE SHAPING
Dec 1 st each side on next row, then every 8th row 9 times more— 90 (100, 110, 120) sts. Work even until piece measures 21"/53.5cm from beg, end with a WS row.

ARMHOLE SHAPING
Bind off 4 (5, 6, 7) sts at beg of next 2 rows. Dec 1 st each side on next row, then every other row 1 (3, 4, 5) times more—78 (82, 88, 94) sts. Work even until armhole measures 8½ (9, 9½, 10)"/21.5 (23, 24, 25.5)cm, end with a WS row.

SHOULDER AND NECK SHAPING
Bind off 7 (7, 8, 9) sts at beg of next 2 rows, then 6 (7, 8, 9) sts at beg of next 4 rows. AT THE SAME TIME, bind off center 36 sts. Working both sides at once, dec 1 st from each neck edge *every* row twice.

LEFT FRONT
With smaller needles, cast on 54 (59, 64, 69) sts. Work in rib pat as foll:
Row 1 (RS) K3, *p2, k3; rep from *, end k1.
Row 2 P4, *k2, p3; rep from * to end.

Rep rows 1 and 2 for 3"/7.5cm, inc 0 (1, 0, 1) st in center of last row and end with a RS row—54 (60, 64, 70) sts. Change to larger needles. **Set-up row (WS)** P11, pm, k2, p18, k2, pm, p 21 (27, 31, 37).

BEG CHART PAT I
Row 1 (RS) K1, work in bamboo st across next 20 (26, 30, 36) sts, sl marker, work 22 sts of chart, sl marker, work in bamboo st across next 10 sts, k1. Cont to foll chart in this way to row 12, then rep rows 1–12 for cable pat. AT THE SAME TIME, cont to work rem sts in bamboo st as established. Work even until piece measures 5"/12.5cm from beg, end with a WS row.

SIDE SHAPING
Dec 1 st at side edge on next row, then every 8th row 9 times more—44 (50, 54, 60) sts. Work even until piece measures same length as back to underarm, end with a WS row.

ARMHOLE SHAPING
Bind off 4 (5, 6, 7) sts at beg of next row. Work next row even. Dec 1 st from armhole edge on next row, then every other row 1 (3, 4, 5) times more—38 (41, 43, 47) sts. Work even until armhole measures 5½ (6, 6½, 7)"/14 (15, 16.5, 17.5)cm, end with a RS row.

NECK SHAPING
Bind off 7 (8, 7, 8) sts at beg of next row. Dec 1 st from neck edge on next row, then *every* row 11 times more—19 (21, 24, 27) sts. Work even until piece measures

same length as back to shoulder, end with a WS row.

SHOULDER SHAPING
Bind off 7 (7, 8, 9) sts at armhole edge once, then 6 (7, 8, 9) sts twice.

RIGHT FRONT
With smaller needles, cast on 54 (59, 64, 69) sts. Work in rib pat as foll:
Row 1 (RS) K4, *p2, k3; rep from * to end.
Row 2 P, *k2, p3; rep from *, end p1.
Rep rows 1 and 2 for 3"/7.5cm, inc 0 (1, 0, 1) st in center of last row and end with a RS row—54 (60, 64, 70) sts. Change to larger needles. **Set-up row (WS)** P 21 (27, 31, 37), pm, k2, p18, k2, pm, p11.

BEG CHART PAT II
Row 1 (RS) K1, work in bamboo st across next 10 sts, sl marker, work 22 sts of chart, sl marker, work in bamboo st across next 20 (26, 30, 36) sts, k1. Cont to foll chart in this way to row 12, then rep rows 1–12 for cable pat. AT THE SAME TIME, cont to work rem sts in bamboo st as established. Work even until piece measures 5"/12.5cm from beg, end with a WS row. Cont to work same as left front, reversing all shaping.

SLEEVES
With smaller needles, cast on 55 sts. Work in rib pat for 3"/7.5cm, inc 3 sts evenly spaced across last row and end with a RS row—58 sts. Change to larger needles. Purl next row. Cont in bamboo st and work

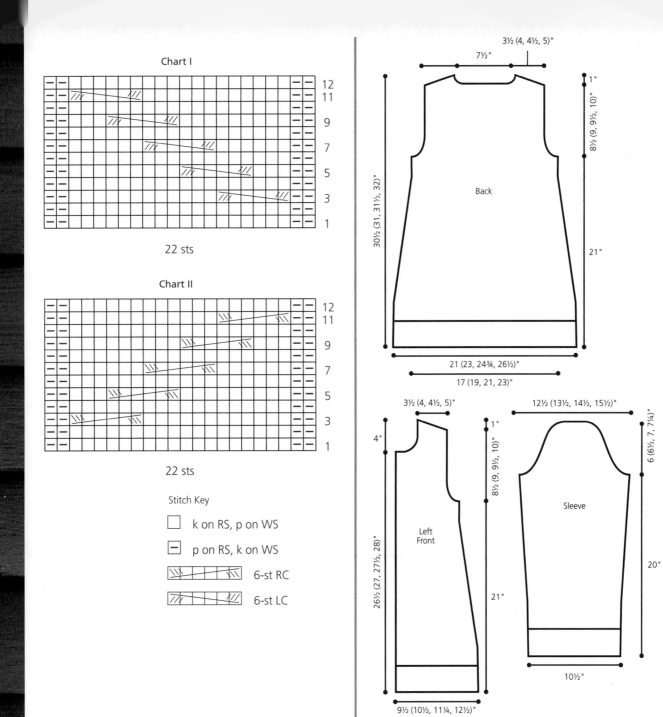

Chart I

22 sts

Chart II

22 sts

Stitch Key

☐ k on RS, p on WS

⊟ p on RS, k on WS

6-st RC

6-st LC

Back

3½ (4, 4½, 5)"

7½"

1"

8½ (9, 9½, 10)"

21"

30½ (31, 31½, 32)"

21 (23, 24¾, 26½)"

17 (19, 21, 23)"

Left Front

3½ (4, 4½, 5)"

4"

1"

8½ (9, 9½, 10)"

21"

26½ (27, 27½, 28)"

9½ (10½, 11¼, 12½)"

7½ (8½, 9½, 10½)"

Sleeve

12½ (13½, 14½, 15½)"

6 (6½, 7, 7¼)"

20"

10½"

even for 2"/5cm, end with a WS row. Inc 1 st each side on next row, then every 24th (14th, 8th, 6th) row 3 (5, 8, 11) times more—66 (70, 76, 82) sts. Work even until piece measures 20"/51cm from beg, end with a WS row.

CAP SHAPING

Bind off 4 (5, 6, 7) sts at beg of next 2 rows. Dec 1 st each side on next row, then every other row 12 (13, 14, 15) times more, then *every* row 8 times. Bind off rem 16 (16, 18, 20) sts.

DETACHABLE HOOD

With larger needles, cast on 62 sts. Knit next 4 rows.
Next (buttonhole) row (RS) K12, *bind off next 2 sts, k10; rep from * twice more, end, bind off next 2 sts, k12.
Next row Knit across, casting on 2 sts over bound-off sts. Knit next 4 rows. Cont in bamboo st as foll:
Row 1 (RS) K1, [yo, k2, pass yo over 2 sts on RH needle] 14 times, pm, k4, pm, [yo, k2, pass yo over 2 sts on RH needle] 14 times, k1.
Row 2 Purl.

BACK SHAPING

Inc row (RS) Work to first marker, M1, sl marker, k4, sl marker, M1, work to end—64 sts. Working new sts into bamboo st, rep inc row every 4th row 8 times more, then every other row twice—84 sts.
Dec row (RS) Work to 2 sts before first marker, k2tog, sl marker, k4, sl marker, ssk, work to end—82 sts. Rep dec row every other row 13 times more. Bind off rem 56 sts.

FINISHING

Lightly block piece to measurements. Sew shoulders seams.

LEFT FRONT BAND

With RS facing and circular needle, pick up and k 118 (120, 123, 125) sts evenly spaced along left front edge.
Row 1 (WS) P 3 (4, 3, 4), *k3, p3; rep from *, end p 0 (1, 0, 1).
Row 2 K 3 (4, 3, 4), *p3, k3; rep from *, end k 0 (1, 0, 1).
Rep rows 1 and 2 eight times more, then row 1 once. Bind off in rib pat.

RIGHT FRONT BAND

Work same as left front band.

NECKBAND

With RS facing and circular needle, pick up and k 33 sts along right front neck to right shoulder seam, 37 sts along back neck edge to left shoulder seam, then 33 sts along left front neck edge—103 sts.
Row 1 (WS) P3, *k2, p3; rep from * to end.
Row 2 K3, *p2, k3; rep from * to end. Rep rows 1 and 2 four times more. Bind off in rib pat.
Sew hood seam.

HOOD BAND

With RS facing and circular needle, pick up and k 128 sts evenly spaced across front edge of hood.
Cont in rib pat as foll:
Row 1 (WS) P3, *k2, p3; rep from * to end.
Row 2 K3, *p2, k3; rep from * to end. Cont in rib pat for 3 rows more.
Next (buttonhole) row (RS) K3, bind off next 2 sts, work in rib to last 5 sts, bind off next 2 sts, work to end. **Next row** Work in rib pat, casting-on 2 sts over bound-off sts. Cont in rib pat for 2 rows more. Bind off loosely in rib pat.

LOOPS AND TOGGLE

LOOPS (MAKE 10)
Make a slipknot 3"/7.5cm from end of yarn. Place on hook, ch 40. Cut yarn, leaving a 3"/7.5cm tail. Fasten off. Place markers for 5 loops along ditch line between right front edge and right front band, with the first 2½"/6.5cm from lower edge, the last 3"/7.5cm from top edge of neckband and the others evenly spaced between. Using tails, sew each loop in ditch, having ends side by side. Place markers for 5 toggles along ditch line between left front edge and left front band same as right front. Thread each rem loop through a toggle. Using tails, sew each toggle in ditch, having ends side by side. Place markers for 5 snaps on WS of right front band and RS of left front band, with the first 2½"/6.5cm from lower edge, the last 3"/7.5cm from top edge of neckband and the others evenly spaced between. Centering snap halves on front bands, sew top half of each snap to WS of right front band and bottom half to RS of left front band. For hood, place markers for 2 buttons along ditch line between neck edge and neckband, with the first and last 5"/12.5cm from front edges. Sew on buttons. Attach hood, then mark for rem 4 buttons. Detach hood. Sew on rem buttons. ●

■ QUINCE & CO.

A small company with big plans

Company Stats

COMPANY STARTED
2010

PROPRIETORS
Pam Allen, Carrie Bostick
Hoge and Bob Rice

LOCATION
Portland, Maine

YARNS
Four types of wool yarn,
with fiber from the United
States at the core

BUSINESS PHILOSOPHY

*To use domestic fiber
when possible and
source fibers from other
countries where they
can identify the origins
and/or get organic,
earth-friendly goods.*

WEBSITE
quinceandco.com

Quince & Co. is the result of one too many "Wouldn't it be great if…" conversations among three yarnophiles. Comprised of two knitwear designers and an owner of a spinning mill, all of whom have a strong bias toward natural fibers, Quince & Co. has created a line of thoughtfully conceived yarns. The yarns are spun from American wool or sourced from overseas suppliers who grow plants, raise animals, or manufacture a yarn in as earth- and labor-friendly a way as possible. In short, Quince & Co. thinks they can have their yarn and knit it, too.

With a roster including Pam Allen, who was editor of *Interweave Knits* from 2003–2007 and more recently worked as creative director at Classic Elite Yarns; Carrie Bostick Hoge, a knitter, photographer and designer; and Bob Rice, who rescued a historic mill from steady decline, this young company knows its yarn.

The fiber Quince & Co. uses comes from merino, Rambouillet, and Columbia-based sheep that roam the ranges of Montana and Wyoming. All their wool and wool-blend yarns are spun in a New England mill with a venerable history. By sourcing the wool in the United States and manufacturing the yarn locally, they minimize their carbon footprint.

Textiles were once a huge industry in New England. Quince & Co. is surrounded by mill buildings that are empty or being turned into upscale condominiums or corporate offices. Pam, Carrie and Bob love the idea of working with a mill that's generations old and still churning out great yarn on early twentieth-century equipment.

However, as much as they wish to promote American sheep and yarns, they also want to enjoy the pleasures of fibers that aren't readily available in the United States. When they blend their wool with other fibers, they find out as much as possible where and how those fibers came to be. If sourcing a yarn from a plant fiber, they want to know if it was grown in conditions that are healthy for the soil and for those who tend and harvest it. If they're looking for an animal fiber, they want to know if the animal was raised in a way that sustains the earth and preserves the culture of the people who raise it.

Quince & Co. began as a (mostly) online yarn company. Initially, Quince will be available in Knitwit, a Portland, Maine, yarn store, with hopes to expand into other stores around the country.

1. Vintage spools
2. An antique scale
3. Historic mill equipment

QUINCE & CO.

Lily-of-the-Valley Shrug

SIZES
Instructions are written for Small. Changes for Medium, Large and X-Large are in parentheses.

FINISHED MEASUREMENTS
BUST 32 (36, 40, 44)"/81 (91.5, 101.5, 111.5)cm
LENGTH 11½ (12, 12½, 13)"/29 (30.5, 31.5, 33)cm
UPPER ARM 14½ (15½, 16½, 17½)"/37 (39.5, 42, 44.5)cm

MATERIALS
■ 4 (5, 5, 6) 1¾oz/50g hanks (each approx 181yd/166m) of Quince & Co. *Chickadee* (American wool) in #203 frost (4)
■ Sportweight scrap yarn in a contrasting color
■ One pair size 5 (3.75mm) needles *or size to obtain gauge*
■ Size 5 (3.75mm) circular needle, 32"/81cm long
■ Stitch holders
■ Stitch markers

GAUGE
24 sts and 34 rows to 4"/10cm over St st using size 5 (3.75mm) needles.
Take time to check gauge.

Allen was taken by the lace pieces in Nancy Bush's book *Knitted Lace of Estonia* (Interweave Press, 2008), in particular the lily-of-the-valley patterns. She wanted to use one of the variations around the neck of her little shrug, but didn't want the piece to get too fussy by adding the same border to the sleeves. Instead, she centered a single motif of lily-of-the-valley buds juxtaposed with a leaf on a borderless cuff.

NOTES
1) Shrug is made in two halves, each beg at the cuff and ending at center back.
2) When working chart II, always read chart from right to left.

STITCH GLOSSARY
N (make nupp) Working *very loosely*, work ([k1, yo] twice, k1) in next st.

RIGHT HALF
SLEEVE
With straight needles, cast on 22 (22, 25, 25), pm, cast on 21 sts, pm, cast on 22 (22, 25, 25) sts—65 (65, 71, 71) sts.

BEG CHART PAT I
Row 1 (RS) K 22 (22, 25, 25), sl marker, work 21 sts of chart, sl marker, k 22 (22, 25, 25).

Row 2 P 22 (22, 25, 25), sl marker, work 21 sts of chart, sl marker, p 22 (22, 25, 25). Keeping sts each side of markers in St st, cont to foll chart in this way to row 14, then rep rows 1–14 once more, dropping markers on last row. Cont in St st on all sts until piece measures 5"/12.5cm from beg, end with a WS row.
Inc row (RS) K2, M1, knit to last 2 sts, M1, k2. Rep inc row every 12th (8th, 8th, 8th) row 3 (4, 4, 4) times more, every 6th row once, every 4th row 1 (2, 2, 3) times, then every other row 5 (6, 6, 8) times—87 (93, 99, 105) sts. Work even until piece measures 12 (12, 12½, 13)"/30.5 (30.5, 31.5, 33)cm from beg, end with a WS row.

SIDE SHAPING
Cast on 2 sts at beg of next 4 rows, 4 sts at beg of next 2 rows, then 6 sts at beg of next 2 rows—115 (121, 127, 133) sts. Work even for 1 (2, 3, 4)"/2.5 (5, 7.5, 10)cm, end with a WS row.

FRONT SHAPING
Dec row (RS) Ssk, knit to end. Rep dec row every 6th row twice more, then every other row 5 times, end with a WS row. Bind off 2 sts at beg of next 3 RS rows, 4 sts at beg of next RS row, then 40 (43, 46, 49) sts at beg of next RS row—57 (60, 63, 66) sts.

BACK
Work even for 3½"/9cm, end with a WS row. Place rem 57 (60, 63, 66) sts on holder.

LEFT HALF
Work same as right half to front shaping.

FRONT SHAPING
Dec row (RS) Knit to last 2 sts, k2tog. Rep dec row every 6th row twice more, then every other row 5 times, end with a RS row. Bind off 2 sts at beg of next 3 WS rows, 4 sts at beg of next WS row, then 40 (43, 46, 49) sts at beg of next RS row—57 (60, 63, 66) sts.

BACK
Work even for 3½"/9cm, end with a WS row.
Place rem 57 (60, 63, 66) sts on holder.

FINISHING
Block piece to measurements.
To join back, place 57 (60, 63, 66) sts from right back holder on a straight needle ready for a RS row, then place 57 (60, 63, 66) sts from left back holder on a straight needle ready for a WS row.
With WS tog (seam will be on the RS), cont to work 3-needle bind-off. Sew side and sleeve seams.

BORDER
Beg at lower center back seam, place contrasting yarn marker every 2⅛"/5.5cm around entire perimeter of shrug—23 (25, 28, 30) sections. With RS facing and circular needle, pick up and k 13 sts between each pair of markers—299 (325, 364, 390) sts.
Remove yarn markers. Join and pm for beg of rnds.

BEG CHART PAT II
Rnd 1 Work 13-st rep 23 (25, 28, 30) times. Cont to foll chart in this way to rnd 14. Bind off all sts loosely purlwise. Lightly block border. ●

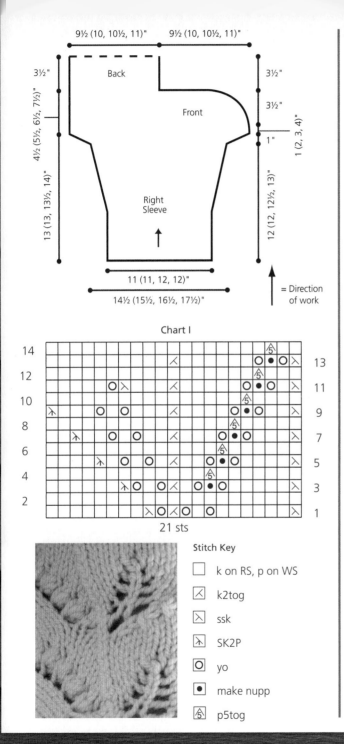

9½ (10, 10½, 11)"   9½ (10, 10½, 11)"

3½"   Back

3½"

Front

3½"

4½ (5½, 6½, 7½)"

1"

1 (2, 3, 4)"

13 (13, 13½, 14)"

Right Sleeve

12 (12, 12½, 13)"

11 (11, 12, 12)"

14½ (15½, 16½, 17½)"

↑ = Direction of work

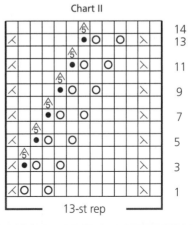

Chart I

14
12
10
8
6
4
2

13
11
9
7
5
3
1

21 sts

Stitch Key

☐	k on RS, p on WS
⤢	k2tog
⤡	ssk
⅄	SK2P
O	yo
●	make nupp
⑤	p5tog

Chart II

14
13
11
9
7
5
3
1

13-st rep

■ SWANS ISLAND YARNS

Beautiful yarn...naturally

Company Stats

COMPANY STARTED
1992; Swans Island Yarns
founded in 2009

PROPRIETOR
Bill Laurita

LOCATION
Northport, Maine

YARNS
Two types, both made in the
United States

BUSINESS PHILOSOPHY

To provide beautifully styled natural products.

WEBSITE
swansislandyarns.com

Known for their high-quality handwoven blankets, throws, scarves and other products for over 15 years, Swans Island Blankets, which produces Swans Island Yarns, is a Maine-based textile company owned by Bill Laurita.

Featured in the national media—including *Martha Stewart Living, Coastal Living, Vogue* and *The New York Times*—and the recipient of a craft excellence award from the Smithsonian Institute, Swans Island began their yarn business after customers began asking for the fiber the blankets were woven from.

The yarn is dyed using natural substances such as indigo plant and cochineal shells—the same substances that are used for Swans Island woven goods. The yarn is dyed in the skein with a labor-intensive method that involves gently dipping each skein into a kettle, saturating it with dye and then allowing it to air-dry. This process leads to yarns that are loftier and softer than other quicker dyeing methods, producing colors containing beautiful variegation, just like what is seen in nature. Completely made in Maine and certified organic, Swans Island yarns exhibit a natural, unique look.

Swans Island often hosts tours of the loom and dye houses for design, textile, fiber, knitting and weaving enthusiasts, and just this year opened a new, larger dye house. They even have a high-profile supporter in Michelle Obama, who recently purchased a gift for the prime minister of Ireland from them. Quickly becoming known for their production methods, this company is one to watch.

1. Moving the flock
2. Sorting the fleece
3. Dyeing the yarn with natural ingredients
4. Home office
5. Penned up

■ SWANS ISLAND YARNS

Maritime Hat and Mitten Set

NORTHEAST

SIZE
Instructions are written
for one size.

FINISHED MEASUREMENTS
HAT
HEAD CIRCUMFERENCE
18"/45.5cm
DEPTH 8"/20.5cm)
MITTENS
HAND CIRCUMFERENCE
7¼"/18.5cm
LENGTH OF CUFF
approx 1"/2.5cm

MATERIALS
■ 1 3½oz/100g hank
(each approx 250yd/229m) of
Swans Island Yarns *Worsted*
(wool) each in green (MC) and
indigo (CC) (4)
■ One pair each sizes 7 and 8
(4.5 and 5mm) needles *or size to
obtain gauge*
■ Stitch holders
■ Stitch markers

GAUGE
22 sts and 23 rows to 4"/10cm
over St st and Fair Isle pats using
larger needles.
Take time to check gauge.

Jil Eaton learned to knit when she
was 4 years old and grew up in
Maine where hand-knits are
cherished and classic maritime
patterns have been passed down
through generations. The
stranded colorwork pattern
creates a fabric that is warm and
durable, perfect for chilly New
England winters.

NOTE
When working Fair Isle patterns,
hold MC and CC in separate hands
(one Continental and one English)
to knit patterns more quickly.

STITCH GLOSSARY
Kf&b To inc 1 st, and maintain Fair
Isle pat, knit into the front of next st
using the next color, then in the
back of the same st using the
following color.

FAIR ISLE PATTERN I
(over an odd number of sts)
Row 1 (RS) K1 MC, *k1 CC, k1 MC;
rep from * to end.
Row 2 P1 CC, *p1 MC, p1 CC;
rep from * to end.
Rep rows 1 and 2 for Fair Isle pat I.

FAIR ISLE PATTERN II
(over an even number of sts)
Row 1 (RS) *K1 MC, k1 CC; rep
from * to end.
Row 2 *P1 MC, p1 CC;
rep from * to end.

Rep rows 1 and 2 for Fair Isle pat II.

HAT
With smaller needles and MC, cast
on 99 sts. Work in St st for 10 rows.
Change to larger needles. Cont in
Fair Isle pat I for 6½"/16.5cm,
end with a WS row.

CROWN SHAPING
Dec row 1 (RS) With MC, *k2tog;
rep from *, end k1—50 sts.
Next row *P1 MC, p1 CC; rep from
* to end.
Dec row 2 (RS) With MC, *k2tog;
rep from * to end—25 sts.
Next row P1 CC, *p1 MC, p1 CC;
rep from * to end.
Dec row 3 (RS) With MC, *k2tog;
rep from *, end k1—13 sts.
Next row P1 CC, *p1 MC, p1 CC;
rep from * to end.
Rep last 2 rows once more—7 sts.
Cut MC, leaving an 18"/45.5cm
tail. Thread through rem sts. Pull
tog tightly and secure end, then
sew back seam, reversing seam over
bottom 1"/2.5cm.

MITTENS

CUFF

With smaller needles and MC, cast on 40 sts. Work in St st for 10 rows. Change to larger needles. Cont in Fair Isle pat II for 2"/5cm, end with a RS row.

THUMB GUSSET

Next row (WS) Work 18 sts, pm, work 4 sts, pm, work rem 18 sts.
Inc row (RS) Working new sts into Fair Isle pat II, work to first marker, sl marker, kf&b, work to 1 st before second marker, kf&b, sl marker, work to end—42 sts (6 sts between markers). Work next row even. Rep last 2 rows 3 times more, then inc row once, end with a RS row—50 sts (14 sts between markers).
Next row (WS) Work to first marker and place these 18 sts on holder, work 14 thumb sts, work rem 18 sts and place on a second holder. Cut yarns.

THUMB

Next row (RS) Rejoin yarns and cont to work even in Fair Isle pat II on 14 sts for 2"/5cm, end with a WS row. Cut CC.
Next row (RS) With MC, k2tog across—7 sts. Cut MC, leaving a 10"/25.5cm tail. Thread through rem sts. Pull tog tightly and secure end, then sew thumb seam.

HAND

Place sts on holders back to LH needle ready for a RS row—36 sts.

Rejoin yarns.
Next row (RS) Work across first 18 sts, keeping to color changes, pick up and k 4 sts evenly spaced across base of thumb, work across last 18 sts—40 sts. Work even until hand measures approx 4¾"/12cm from base of thumb, end with a WS row.

TOP SHAPING

Dec row (RS) With MC, *k2tog; rep from * to end—20 sts.
Next row *P1 MC, p1 CC; rep from * to end. Rep last 2 rows once more, then dec row once more—5 sts. Cut MC, leaving an 18"/45.5cm tail. Thread through rem sts. Pull tog tightly and secure end, then sew side seam, reversing seam over bottom ½"/1.5cm. ●

■ KRAEMER YARNS

Small-town heroes

Company Stats

COMPANY STARTED
1907; yarn line started in 2005

PROPRIETOR
David Schmidt

LOCATION
Nazareth, Pennsylvania

YARNS
Seventeen types, all made in the United States

BUSINESS PHILOSOPHY
To build meaningful relationships with our employees and customers to create innovative spun yarns.

WEBSITE
kraemeryarns.com

Kraemer Yarns sits proudly on Main Street in Nazareth, Pennsylvania, a living, breathing testament to small-town America.

Kraemer recently celebrated their one-hundredth anniversary, and a single family has overseen the company for its entire history. Currently run by the fourth generation of Kraemers, the company has more than 60 employees.

Kraemer spins approximately 30,000 pounds of yarn each week, supplying the craft, apparel, home furnishing, industrial and hand knitting markets with a wide range of products, including carpet, apparel and rope. They began producing their own line of handknitting yarns in 2005. Spun from natural and synthetic fibers, these include "Sterling Silk & Silver," one of the most unique yarns produced by Kraemer. It is a blend of merino wool, silk, nylon and real silver spun as a sock yarn but appropriate for any garment where a little sparkle is desired.

Kraemer Yarns uses U.S. sources when possible. One such supplier is Stotts Ranch from the Texas Hill Country, which produces high-quality mohair and merino fibers.

1. Fleece ready for processing
2. Making yarn
3. Ready for color!

NORTHEAST

■ KRAEMER YARNS

Purple Mountains Majesty Shawl

■■■■▶

FINISHED MEASUREMENTS
Approx 88" x 40"/223.5cm x 101.5cm

MATERIALS
■ 3 3.5oz/100g hanks (each approx 420yd/384m) of Kraemer Yarns *Sterling Silk & Silver* (superwash merino/silk/nylon/silver) in #Y1408 purple plush ❶
■ Size 7 (4.5mm) circular needle, 32"/81cm long *or size to obtain gauge*
■ One 1mm beading crochet hook
■ Size 6/0 glass beads: 75 in silver-lined light amethyst, 375 in silver-lined blue, 525 in silver-lined gold, 625 in silver-lined crystal and 775 in silver-lined lime green

GAUGE
19 sts and 26 rows to 4"/10cm over St st using size 7 (4.5mm) circular needle (before blocking). 14 sts and 20 rows to 4"/10cm over St st using size 7 (4.5mm) circular needle (after blocking).
Take time to check gauges.

This shimmering shawl is inspired by the grandeur of America's many beautiful mountain ranges. The beads represent mountains (amethyst), snow (silver-lined crystal), trees (green), rivers (blue) and stars (gold). Awe-inspiring mountain peaks capped with snow, a deep, bountiful forest and a sparkling stream, all magnified by big, bright stars—this elegant wrap has them all!

NOTE
Shawl is worked from the top down.

STITCH GLOSSARY
Add Bead Slip bead onto shank of crochet hook. With hook facing you, slip next st from LH needle onto crochet hook. Hold taut. Slip bead onto st. Slip st back to LH needle and knit (or purl) it according to chart pat.

SHAWL
Cast on 5 sts. Knit 1 row.

BEG CHART I
NOTES Chart I is worked twice. The 2 sts in garter st each side and the single St st in center are not shown on chart. WS rows are also not shown on chart. All beads are added on RS rows.
Row 1 (RS) K2, yo for chart row 1,

k1 for center st, yo for chart row 1, k2.
Row 2 and all WS rows K2, purl to last 2 sts, k2. Cont to foll chart in this way to row 52—107 sts.

BEG CHART II
NOTES Chart II is worked twice. The 2 sts in garter st at each side and single St st in center are not shown on chart. WS rows are also not shown on chart. All beads are added on RS rows.
Row 53 (RS) K2, work chart row 53, k1, work chart row 53, k2.
Row 54 and all WS rows K2, purl to last 2 sts, k2. Cont to foll chart in this way to row 86—175 sts. To cont chart II, work as foll:
Row 87 (RS) K2, work chart row 87 to rep line, work 34-st rep twice, work to end of chart, k1, work chart row 87 to rep line, work 34-st rep twice, work to end of chart, k2.
Row 88 and all WS rows K2, purl to last 2 sts, k2. Cont to foll chart in this way to row 120—243 sts.

BEG CHART III
NOTES Chart III is worked twice. The 2 sts in garter st at each side and single St st in center are not shown on chart. WS rows are shown on chart. Beads are added on WS rows.
Row 121 (RS) K2, work chart row 121 to rep line, work 34-st rep 3 times, work to end of chart, k1,

work chart row 121 to rep line, work 34-st rep 3 times, work to end of chart, k2. Cont to foll chart in this way to row 174—351 sts. Do *not* cut yarn.

BORDER
With RS facing, cast on 18 sts.

BEG CHART IV
NOTES The last dec on RS rows is worked with 1 st from the newly cast-on border sts and 1 st from the shawl. WS rows are shown on chart. Beads are added on WS rows.
Row 1 (RS) Yo, k4tog, [yo, ssk] 3 times, k1, k2tog, [yo, ssk] 3 times, working last ssk with last border st and 1 st from shawl. Cont to foll chart in this way to row 12, then rep rows 1–12 until all shawl sts are bound off, then bind off border sts.

FINISHING
Block shawl to measurements. ●

Chart I

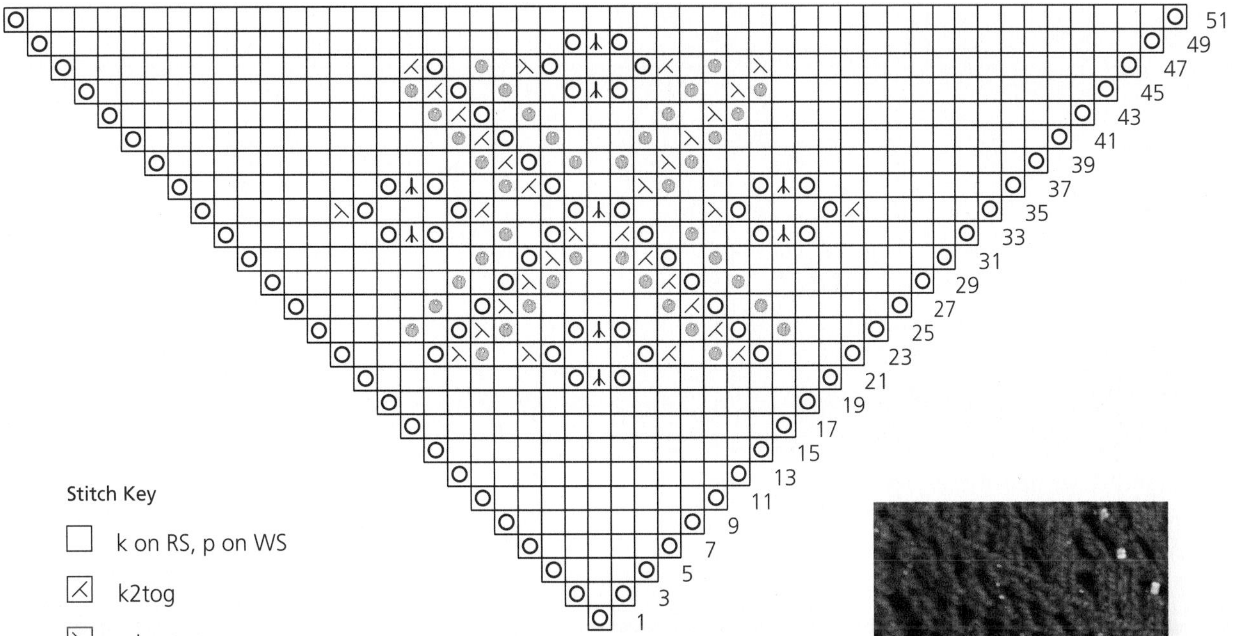

Chart I (knitting chart, rows numbered 1–51 odd)

Stitch Key

☐	k on RS, p on WS
⟋	k2tog
⟍	ssk
◎	yo
⋏	S2KP
⋁	sl 1 purlwise
ⓐ	k4tog

Bead Key

⦿	silver-lined light amethyst
⦿	silver-lined blue
⦿	silver-lined gold
⦿	silver-lined crystal
⦿	silver-lined lime green

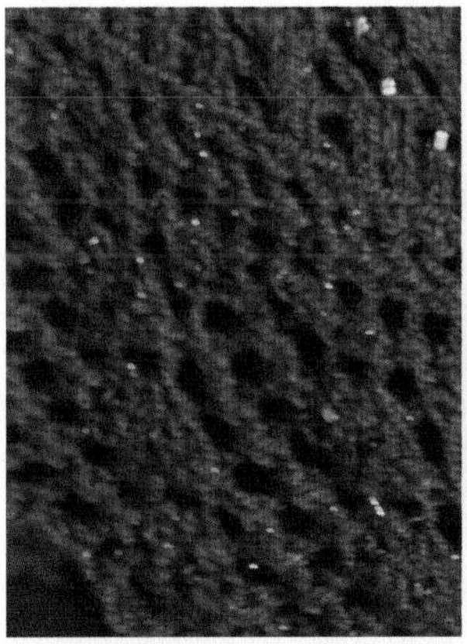

Chart IV

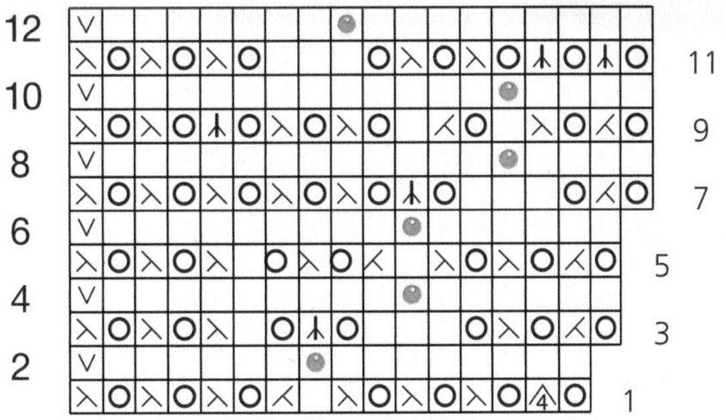

Chart IV (knitting chart, rows numbered 1–12)

Chart II – Part B

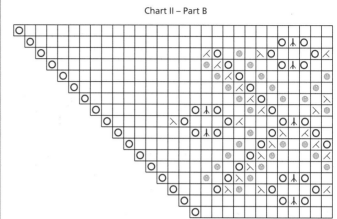

Stitch Key

	k on RS, p on WS
◿	k2tog
◺	ssk
O	yo
⋏	S2KP
V	sl 1 purlwise
⚠	k4tog

Bead Key

◉	silver-lined light amethyst
◉	silver-lined blue
◉	silver-lined gold
◉	silver-lined crystal
◉	silver-lined lime green

Chart II – Part A

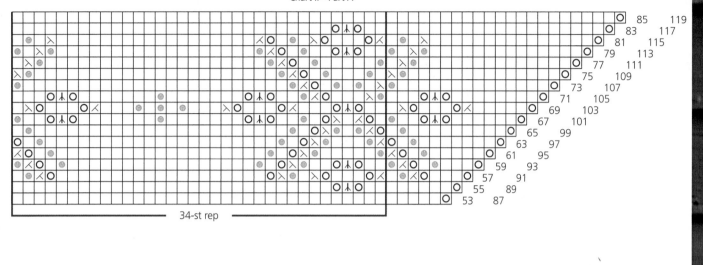

85 119
83 117
81 115
79 113
77 111
75 109
73 107
71 105
69 103
67 101
65 99
63 97
61 95
59 93
57 91
55 89
53 87

34-st rep

Chart III

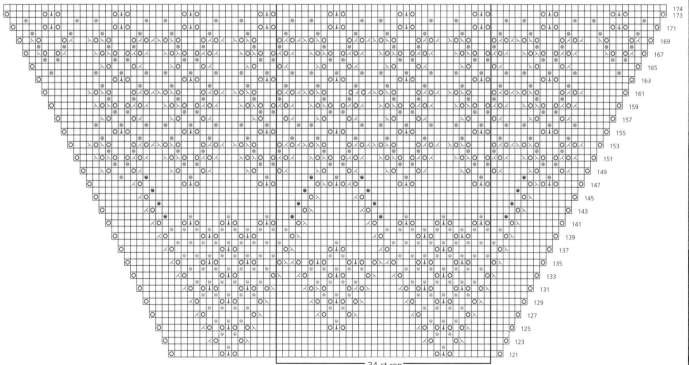

174
173
171
169
167
165
163
161
159
157
155
153
151
149
147
145
143
141
139
137
135
133
131
129
127
125
123
121

34-st rep

■ BROOKLYN TWEED

A classic in the making

Company Stats

COMPANY STARTED
2010

PROPRIETOR
Jared Flood

LOCATION
Brooklyn, New York

YARNS
One woolen-spun 2-ply worsted-weight wool, spun in the United States from domestic wool

BUSINESS PHILOSOPHY
To help knitters procure wools of high quality that directly support farmers, mills and designers from our own backyard.

WEBSITE
brooklyntweed.net

Brooklyn Tweed is dedicated to developing one exquisite, versatile wool yarn, crafted using time-honored methods and sourced from American sheep and mills.

"Shelter" is a worsted-weight wool yarn spun from the wool of Targhee-Columbia sheep raised in the American West. The yarn was developed from the ground up by Jared Flood as an ideal handknitting yarn for classic and traditional knitwear. Each skein of yarn supports the once-great American textile industry.

After learning to knit from his mother at a young age, Flood picked knitting back up in college. Intrigued by sweater construction, traditional knitting techniques and pattern writing, he caught the knitting bug. Following the success of his blog "Brooklyn Tweed," which he started in 2005, and his pattern booklet *Made in Brooklyn,* he began toying with the idea of creating his own line of yarn.

Flood's goal was to find a fiber that had woolly structure and body, could withstand years of wear, and also had the high-quality feel of traditional knitting yarn—all while having a degree of softness that would keep the yarn out of the

"too scratchy" category. After careful consideration, he developed Shelter as a 100-percent-wool yarn made from the Targhee-Columbia crossbreed.

A cross between Targhee and Columbia sheep brings together the sometimes disparate qualities of wearability and durability, creating fibers and yarns that are uniquely suited for the needs of hand knitters and wool-wearers alike.

"Shelter" is spun in historic Harrisville, New Hampshire, where woolen yarns have been produced in the water-powered mills since 1794. These woolen-spun yarns undergo a special preparation process in which fibers are carded by a technique that leaves an amazing amount of air in the finished product. This process creates light yarns that are exceptionally warm and have a rustic aesthetic quality—often sporting a halo and a soft-looking finish.

"Shelter" has a rich palette of seventeen carefully developed heathers that are inspired by the colors of autumn and natural shades of sheep's wool. Because the wool is fleece-dyed, solid shades of color are blended, as if mixing paint, to achieve complex and beautiful colors that give even the simplest fabrics depth and sophistication.

1. The carding machine
2. Spinning frame
3. From cone to hank
4. Antique bobbins

■ BROOKLYN TWEED

Pike's Mitts

■■■■

SIZE
Instructions are written for one size.

FINISHED MEASUREMENTS
Hand circumference 7½"/19cm
Length of cuff approx 1"/2.5cm

MATERIALS
■ 1 1¾oz/50g hank (each approx 140yd/128m) of Brooklyn Tweed *Shelter* (Targhee-Columbia wool) in button jar (**4**)
■ Contrasting worsted-weight yarn (waste yarn)
■ One set (5) each sizes 6 and 7 (4 and 4.5mm) double-pointed needles (dpns) *or size to obtain gauge*
■ Two cable needles (cn)
■ Stitch marker

GAUGE
20 sts and 28 rnds to 4"/10cm over moss st using larger dpns. *Take time to check gauge.*

This particular color of "Shelter" reminds Flood of mossy rocks and texture-filled terrariums. With that in mind, he wanted to design something that had that same feeling of organic texture. Twisted-stitch cable patterns wind like roots and moss and create a nubby texture to cover the palm. While the motifs are the same for each mitt, they are mirrored to create a bit more interest for the knitter and wearer.

NOTES
1) Palm of hand is worked in moss st as shown on chart pat.
2) To work in the rnd, always read charts from right to left.

STITCH GLOSSARY
2-st RC tbl Sl 1 st to cn and hold to *back*, k1 tbl, k1 tbl from cn.
2-st LC tbl Sl 1 st to cn and hold to *front*, k1 tbl, k1 tbl from cn.
2-st RPC tbl Sl 1 st to cn and hold to *back*, k1 tbl, p1 from cn.
2-st LPC tbl Sl 1 st to cn and hold to *front*, p1, k1 tbl from cn.
3-st RPC tbl Sl 1 st to cn and hold to *back*, k2 tbl, p1 from cn.
3-st LPC tbl Sl 2 sts to cn and hold to *front*, p1, k2 tbl from cn.
6-st RC Sl 2 sts to first cn and hold to *back*, sl next 2 sts to 2nd cn and hold to *front*, k2 tbl, k2 tbl from 2nd cn, k2 tbl from first cn.
6-st LC Sl 2 sts to first cn and hold

to *front*, sl next 2 sts to 2nd cn and hold to *back*, k2 tbl, k2 tbl from 2nd cn, k2 tbl from first cn.
Cast on 1 st. Make a firm backward loop onto RH needle.

LEFT MITT
CUFF
With smaller dpn, cast on 38 sts. Divide sts over 4 needles. Join, taking care not to twist sts on needles, pm for beg of rnds.
Rnds 1 and 2 Purl.
Rnd 3 and 4 Knit.
Rnds 5 and 6 Purl.
Rnds 7 and 8 Knit.
Rnds 9 and 10 Purl. Change to larger dpns.
Next (inc) rnd *K9, M1; rep from * to last 2 sts, end k2—42 sts.

BEG CHART PAT
Work rnds 1–31—56 sts.
Rnd 32 Work first 15 sts, place next 15 sts on waste yarn for thumb opening, cast on 3 sts using backward loop cast-on method as shown on chart, work rem 26 sts—44 sts. Cont to foll chart rnds 33–45.
Next (dec) rnd K4, *k2tog, k8—40 sts. Change to smaller dpns. Work rnds 1–6 same as cuff. Bind off purlwise.

Left Mitt

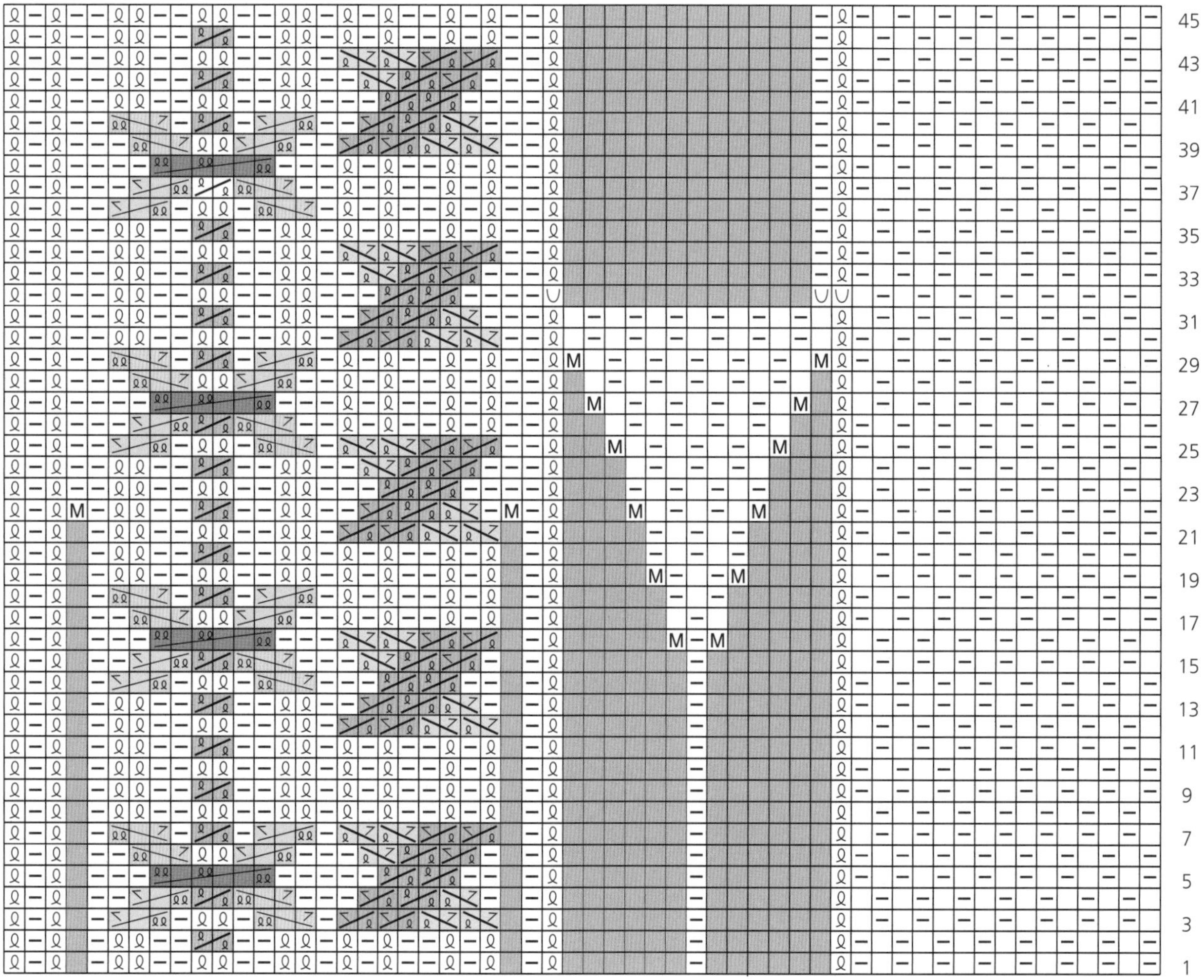

Right Mitt

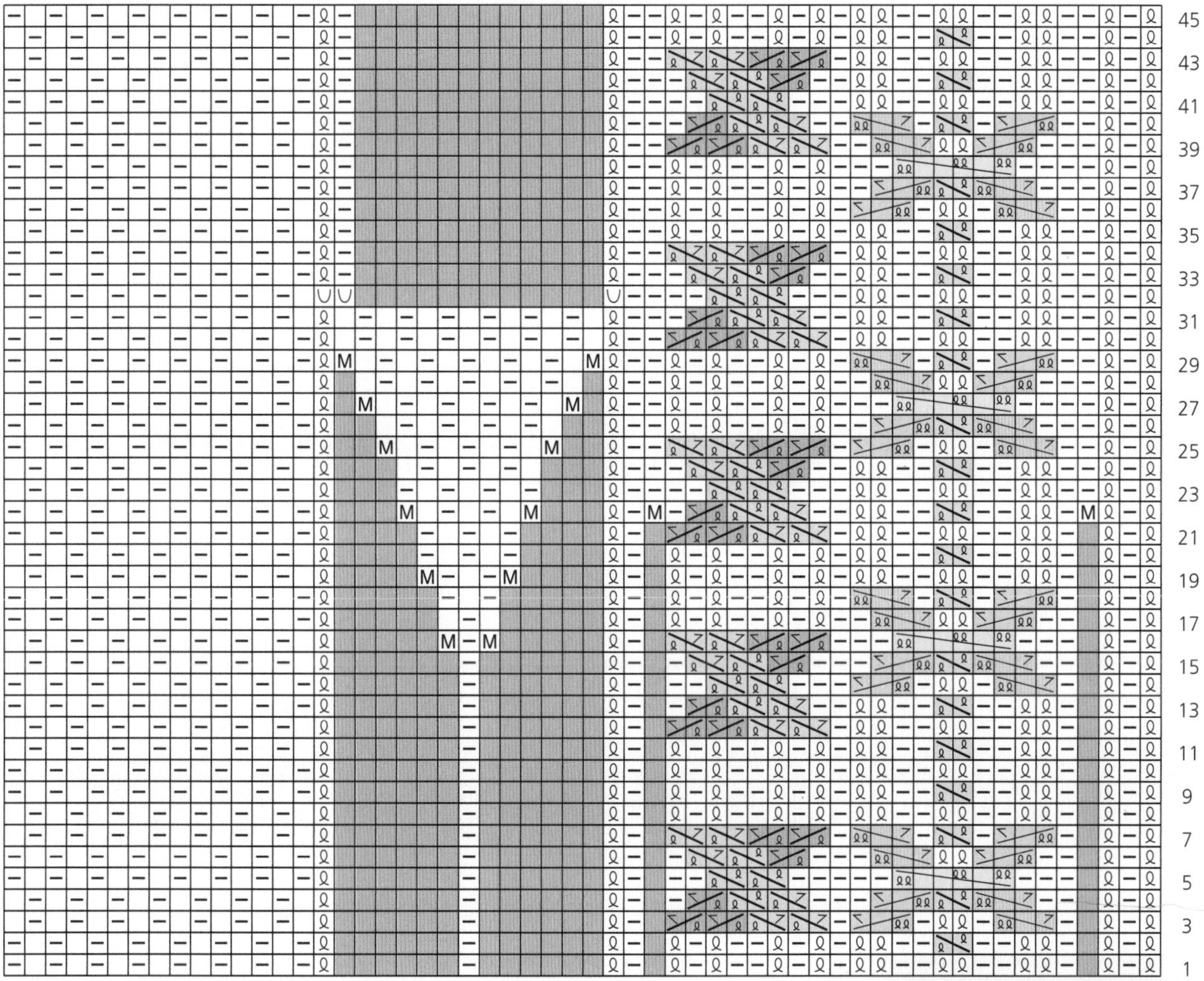

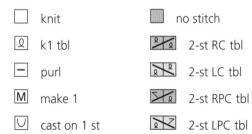

Stitch Key

- knit
- k1 tbl
- purl
- make 1
- cast on 1 st
- no stitch
- 2-st RC tbl
- 2-st LC tbl
- 2-st RPC tbl
- 2-st LPC tbl
- 3-st RPC tbl
- 3-st LPC tbl
- 6-st RC tbl
- 6-st LC tbl

THUMB OPENING
Remove waste yarn and place 15 live sts on 3 smaller dpns (5 sts on each needle). With 4th needle, pick up and k 1 st each of 3 cast-on sts—18 sts. Join and pm for beg of rnds. Work rnds 1–6 same as cuff.

RIGHT MITT
Work same as left mitt to rnd 32—56 sts.

Rnd 32 Work first 26 sts, place next 15 sts on waste yarn for thumb opening, cast on 3 sts using backward loop cast-on method as shown on chart, work rem 15 sts—44 sts. Cont to foll chart rnds 33–45.

Next (dec) rnd *K8, k2tog; rep from * around, end k4—40 sts. Change to smaller dpn. Work rnds 1–6 same as cuff. Bind off purlwise.

THUMB OPENING
Work same as left mitt.

FINISHING
Steam- or wet-block both to finished measurements. Let air-dry. ●

■ KNIT ONE, CROCHET TOO, INC.

A designer's eye for yarn

Company Stats

COMPANY STARTED
1997, then sold and relocated in 2003

PROPRIETOR
Hélène Rush

LOCATION
Windham, Maine

YARNS
Twenty-nine types, one made in the United States

BUSINESS PHILOSOPHY

Rush always selects yarn she herself would like to use, personally trying every sample and putting it through a rigorous evaluation process, making the yarns knitting-owner-approved!

WEBSITE
knitonecrochettoo.com

Hélène Rush first learned to knit from nuns in Montreal in first grade and worked in the design industry for 25 years before purchasing Knit One, Crochet Too in 2003.

A designer for many major knitting magazines, author of five books and former editor of *McCall's Needlework and Crafts* and *Cast On* magazines, Rush looks to garment designs as the inspiration behind her yarn selections.

When evaluating a yarn, Rush imagines the types of garments that would best showcase the fiber; she also designs all the colorways to complement and highlight the personality of the yarn. Attention to detail at every stage and a rigorous testing process are what make this company unique.

As well as carrying almost 30 different yarns, Knit One, Crochet Too is home to the successful Culinary Colors Collection, a ten-bottle dye kit allowing knitters to create their own colorways in their kitchen safely and without exposure to toxins. The company also carries a variety of needle holders, kits, buttons and patterns, many of which are designed by Rush herself.

1. At the mill
2. Prepping for skeins

NORTHEAST

▪ Knit One, Crochet Too, Inc.

East Coast Tunic

▬▬▬▬▶

SIZES
Instructions are written for Small. Changes for Medium, Large and X-Large are in parentheses.

FINISHED MEASUREMENTS
BUST 32 (35, 38, 41)"/81 (89, 96.5, 104)cm
LENGTH 28 (28½, 29, 29½)"/71 (72, 73.5, 75)cm
UPPER ARM 12 (13, 14, 15)"/30.5 (33, 35.5, 38)cm

MATERIALS
▪ 14 (16, 17, 19) .88oz/25g hanks (each approx 88yd/80m) of Knit One, Crochet Too *USDK* (wool) in #819 tan ▨
▪ Size 5 (3.75mm) circular needle, 29"/74cm long *or size to obtain gauge*
▪ One pair size 5 (3.75mm) needles
▪ One set (4) size 5 (3.75mm) double-pointed needles (dpns)
▪ Stitch holders
▪ Stitch marker

GAUGE
30 sts and 36 rows to 4"/10cm over broken twisted rib using size 5 (3.75mm) circular needle.
Take time to check gauge.

NOTE
The knitted fabric will skew. This will be corrected when pieces are blocked.

Coralie Meslin is influenced by the structure and drape of knitted fabric and how it is shaped by fibers, stitchwork and construction. This tunic was inspired by pleated detailing on a woven dress; the pleats create shaping at the front waist and the back is gently shaped with increases and decreases. The yarn has beautiful stitch definition and the wide front and deep back of the neckline provide drama to an otherwise subtle design.

SEED STITCH
(over an odd number of sts)
Row 1 (RS) K1, *p1, k1; rep from * to end.
Row 2 K the purl sts and p the knit sts.
Rep row 2 for seed st.

BROKEN TWISTED RIB
(multiple of 2 sts plus 1)
Row 1 (RS) P1, *k1 tbl, p1; rep from * to end.
Row 2 Knit. Rep rows 1 and 2 for broken twisted rib.

FRONT
With circular needle, cast on 127 (139, 151, 163) sts. Work in seed st for 6 rows. Cont in broken twisted rib and work until piece measures 7"/17.5 from beg, end with a WS row. Dec 1 st each side on next row—125 (137, 149, 161) sts. Work even until piece measures

10"/25.5cm from beg, end with a WS row. Dec 1 st each side on next row—123 (135, 147, 159) sts. Work even until piece measures 11"/28cm from beg, end with a WS row.

SHAPING WAIST AND SET-UP FOR PLEATS
Next (dec) row (RS) Work across first 30 (34, 38, 42) sts, place next 13 sts on a holder and hold in front, work across center 37 (41, 45, 49) sts, place next 13 sts on a holder and hold in front, work across last 30 (34, 38, 42) sts—97 (109, 121, 133) sts. Work even for 2"/5cm, end with a WS row. Leave sts on circular needle. *Do not cut yarn.*

PLEATS
Place sts from first holder on dpn as foll: 3 sts on Needle 1; 7 sts on Needle 2; 3 sts on Needle 3. Holding Needle 2 with RS facing, turn Needles 1 and 3 so they are in back of sts on Needle 2. Join and pm for beg of rnds.
Rnd 1 Needle 1 k3; Needle 2 [k1 tbl, p1] 3 times, k1 tbl; Needle 3 k3.
Rnd 2 Needle 1 k3; Needle 2 p7; Needle 3 k3. Rep rnds 1 and 2 until pleat measures 2"/5cm, end with rnd 2. Place sts from Needle 1 back on holder, then sts from Needles 2 and 3. Work 2nd pleat same as first pleat. Return to sts on circular needle.
Next (joining) row (RS) Keeping to

pat st, work across first 30 (34, 38, 42) sts, then work across next 13 sts on first holder, work across center 37 (41, 45, 49) sts, work across next 13 sts on 2nd holder, then work across last 30 (34, 38, 42) sts—123 (135, 147, 159) sts. Work even until piece measures 14"/35.5cm from beg, end with a WS row. Dec 1 st each side on next row—121 (133, 145, 157) sts. Work even until piece measures 15"/38cm from beg, end with a WS row. Dec 1 st each side on next row—119 (131, 143, 155) sts. Work even until piece measures 20"/51cm from beg, end with a WS row.

CAP SLEEVE SHAPING

Inc 1 st each side on next row, then every other row 9 times more—139 (151, 163, 175) sts. Mark beg and end of last row. Work even until armhole measures 4 (4½, 5, 5½)"/10 (11.5, 12.5, 14) cm above marked row, end with a WS row.

NECK SHAPING

Next row (RS) Work across first 35 (41, 46, 51) sts, join a 2nd ball of yarn and bind off center 69 (69, 71, 73) sts, work to end. Working both sides at once, work next row even. Dec 1 st from each neck edge on next row, then every other row 5 times more—29 (35, 40, 45) sts each side. Work even until armhole measures 6 (6½, 7, 7½)"/15 (16.5, 17.5, 19) above marked row, end with a WS row. Place 29 (35, 40, 45) sts each side on separate holders.

BACK

With circular needle, cast on 127 (139, 151, 163) sts. Work in seed st for 6 rows. Cont in broken twisted rib and work until piece measures 4"/10 from beg, end with a WS row. Dec 1 st each side on next row, then every 6th row 4 times more, then every 4th row 9 times—99 (111, 123, 135) sts. Work even until piece measures 13"/33cm from

beg, end with a WS row. Inc 1 st each side on next row, then every 6th row 9 times more—119 (131, 143, 155) sts. Work even until piece measures 20"/51cm from beg, end with a WS row.

FOR X-SMALL AND SMALL SIZES ONLY
CAP SLEEVE AND NECK SHAPING

Inc 1 st each side on next row, then every other row 3 (6) times more—127 (145) sts.

Next row (RS) Inc 1 st, then work until there are 48 (57) sts on RH needle, join a 2nd ball of yarn and bind off center 33 sts, work across rem sts, inc 1 st at end—48 (57) sts each side. Working both sides at once, work next row even. Cont to inc 1 st each side on next row, then every other row 4 (1) times more. AT THE SAME TIME, dec 1 st from each neck edge on next row, then every other row 23 times more—29 (35) sts each side. Work even until piece measures same length as front to shoulder, end with a WS row. Place 29 (35) sts from each side on separate holders.

FOR MEDIUM AND LARGE SIZES ONLY
CAP SLEEVE SHAPING

Inc 1 st each side on next row, then every other row 9 times more—163 (175) sts. Work even for 0 (4) rows.

NECK SHAPING

Next row (RS) Work across first 64 (69) sts, join a 2nd ball of yarn and bind off center 35 (37) sts, work to end. Working both sides at once, work next row even. Dec 1 st from each neck edge on next row, then every other row 23 times more—40 (45) sts each side. Work even until piece measures same length as front to shoulder, end with a WS row. Place 40 (45) sts from each side on separate holders.

FINISHING
Block pieces to measurements. To join left shoulder, place 29 (35, 40, 45) sts from left front holder on a straight needle ready for a RS row, then place 29 (35, 40, 45) sts from left back holder on a straight needle ready for a RS row. With RS tog, cont to work 3-needle bind-off. Rep for right shoulder.

NECKBAND
With RS facing and circular needle, beg at left shoulder seam, pick up and k 74 (74, 76, 78) sts evenly spaced along front neck edge to right shoulder seam, then pick up and k 104 (104, 106, 108) sts evenly spaced along back neck edge—178 (178, 182, 186) sts. Join and pm for beg of rnd. Cont in seed st as foll:
Rnd 1 *K1, p1; rep from * around.
Rnd 2 K the purl sts and p the knit sts.
Rep rnd 2 four times more. Bind off in seed st.

SLEEVE BANDS
With RS facing and straight needles, pick up and k 85 (91, 97, 105) sts evenly spaced along sleeve edge. Work in seed st for 6 rows. Bind off in seed st. Sew side and sleeve seams. ●

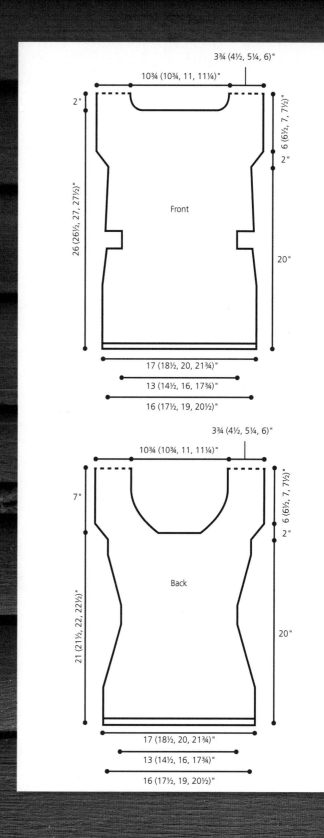

■ GREEN MOUNTAIN SPINNERY

Success through cooperation

Company Stats

COMPANY STARTED
1981

PROPRIETORS
A cooperative comprised of Margaret Atkinson, Maureen Clark, Marshall Gilbert, Gail Haines, Tedd Kapinos, David Ritchie and Judith Robinson. The board of directors also includes founders Libby Mill and Claire Wilson

LOCATION
Putney, Vermont

YARNS
Fourteen types, all made in the United States

BUSINESS PHILOSOPHY
To help sustain sheep farming in the region, and to develop ways to process natural fibers that are friendly to the environment.

WEBSITE
spinnery.com

Since the founding of Green Mountain Spinnery in 1981, and from initial contact with fiber growers through the final labeling and approval of each finished skein of yarn, the Green Mountain Spinnery team attends with care to every step and detail in the yarn-making process.

All the fibers used—alpaca, mohair, wool and organic cotton—are grown in the U.S, and the Spinnery makes every effort to purchase them directly from the growers.

The yarns are created on vintage equipment at a mill in rural Vermont. There is a growing interest in the knitting world in local products and "farm yarns," and Vermont has a reputation as a source of high quality farm products. All workers and pattern designers who create their patterns are local people. The dynamic capabilities of the venerable machinery, combined with the team members' keen understanding of the nuances of each fiber blend, create a superior final product.

The Spinnery was the first custom mill to concentrate on producing yarns that have had no exposure to petroleum products or other chemicals. A Certified Organic processor and currently the only one in New England, the Spinnery produces organic yarns for custom orders as well as their own line of Certified Organic products.

The Spinnery has long been known as a resource for small farmers and specialty fiber producers. Aside from its own custom spinning services, the Spinnery's staff help farmers with issues of flock management for fiber production, and the company is known for its patronage of specialty fibers such as New England–grown alpaca, fine wool and Certified Organic wool.

Entering its 30th year of operation, Green Mountain Spinnery holds on to its commitment to the environment and to sustainability, and that is reflected in their business practices as well as their products. They are a worker-owned cooperative and have a long-term commitment to business sustainability. Both aspects are an important part of how they wish to be viewed by peers in the yarn industry and in the wider business community.

1. An armful of fleece
2. A spectrum of yarn
3. A day at the spinnery

■ GREEN MOUNTAIN SPINNERY

Big Man on Campus Hoodie

■■■■

SIZES
Instructions are written for men's X-Small. Changes for Small, Medium, Large and X-Large are in parentheses

FINISHED MEASUREMENTS
CHEST 37 (40¾, 44½, 46, 49¾)"/94 (103.5, 113, 117, 126.5)cm
LENGTH 23½ (24, 25, 26, 26 ½)"/59.5 (61, 63.5, 66, 67.5)cm
UPPER ARM 13 (14, 15, 16, 17)"/33 (35.5, 38, 40.5, 43)cm

MATERIALS
■ 10, (11, 12, 13, 14) 2oz/57g hanks (each approx 180yd/165m) of Green Mountain Spinnery *Alpaca Elegance* (fine wool/alpaca) in cocoa ⟨3⟩
■ Sizes 5 and 6 (3.75 and 4mm) circular needles, 36"/91cm long *or size to obtain gauge*
■ One pair each size 4 and 5 (3.5 and 3.75mm) needles *or size to obtain gauge*
■ Cable needle (cn)
■ Stitch holders
■ Stitch markers

GAUGE
27 sts and 32 rows to 4"/10cm over body pat st using size 5 (3.75mm) circular needle.
26 sts and 32 rows to 4"/10cm over St st using size 5 (3.75mm) needles. *Take time to check gauge*

The seasonal change from summer to fall—with that certain smell in the air that evokes the first day of school, Friday night football games and marching bands—has always been Bennett's favorite time of year. This sweater is designed to fit an everyday fall lifestyle, whether it be running errands in the morning, passing the football with friends in the afternoon or hanging out at the bonfire.

NOTES
1) Body is worked in one piece to underarms.
2) Body pat st is a combination of vertical columns of 4-st cables and alternating horizontal stripes of St st and reverse St st.
3) Horizontal stripes travel toward the left on each cable twist rnd.

STITCH GLOSSARY
4-st RC Sl next 2 sts to cn and hold to back, k2, k2 from cn.

K1, P1 RIB
(over a multiple of 2 sts plus 1)
Row 1 (RS) K1, *p1, k1; rep from * to end.
Row 2 P1, *k1, p1; rep from * to end. Rep rows 1 and 2 for k1, p1 rib.

BODY
With smaller circular needle, cast on 126 (138, 150, 156, 168) sts, pm

---

(side marker), cast on 126 (138, 150, 156, 168) sts—252 (276, 300, 312, 336) sts. Join, taking care not to twist sts on needle. Place marker for end of rnd and sl marker every rnd.

SET-UP RNDS FOR BODY PAT ST
Slipping markers every rnd, cont as foll:
Rnds 1–5 *P2, k4; rep from * to side marker; *p2, k4; rep from * to end of rnd.

BEG BODY PAT ST
Rnd 1 K6, pm, *p2, 4-st RC; rep from * to side marker; k6, pm, *p2, 4-st RC; rep from * to end of rnd. Slipping markers every rnd, cont as foll:
Rnds 2–8 K6, *p2, k4; rep from * to side marker; k6, *p2, k4; rep from * to end of rnd.
Rnd 9 P8 dropping marker, pm, 4-st RC, *p2, 4-st RC; rep from * to side marker; p8 dropping marker, pm, 4-st RC, *p2, 4-st RC; rep from * to end of rnd. Slipping markers every rnd, cont as foll:
Rnds 10–16 P8, k4, *p2, k4; rep from * to side marker; p8, k4, *p2, k4; rep from * to end of rnd.
Rnd 17 K12 dropping marker, pm, *p2, 4-st RC; rep from * to side marker; k12 dropping marker, pm, *p2, 4-st RC; rep from * to end of rnd. Slipping markers every rnd, cont as foll:
Rnds 18–24 K12, *p2, k4; rep from

* to side marker; k12, *p2, k4; rep from * to end of rnd.
Rnd 25 P14 dropping marker, pm, 4-st RC, *p2, 4-st RC; rep from * to side marker; p14 dropping marker, pm, 4-st RC, *p2, 4-st RC; rep from * to end of rnd. Slipping markers every rnd, cont as foll:
Rnds 26–32 P14, k4, *p2, k4; rep from * to side marker; p14, k4, *p2, k4; rep from * to end of rnd.
Rnd 33 K18 dropping marker, pm, *p2, 4-st RC; rep from * to side marker; k18 dropping marker, pm, *p2, 4-st RC; rep from * to end of rnd. Slipping markers every rnd, cont as foll:
Rnds 34–40 K18, *p2, k4; rep from * to side marker; k18, *p2, k4; rep from * to end of rnd.

Rnd 41 P20 dropping marker, pm, 4-st RC, *p2, 4-st RC; rep from * to side marker; p20 dropping marker, pm, 4-st RC, *p2, 4-st RC; rep from * to end of rnd. Slipping markers every rnd, cont as foll:
Rnds 42–48 P20, k4, *p2, k4; rep from * to side marker; p20, k4, *p2, k4; rep from * to end of rnd. Cont to work in this way, advancing stripes every 8th rnd as foll: advance each St st stripe by 4 sts more than reverse St st stripe below, and advancing each reverse St st stripe by 2 sts more than St st stripe below. Work even until piece measures 16 (16,16½, 17,17)"/40.5 (40.5, 42, 43, 43)cm from beg.

BACK
Change to larger straight needles; leave front sts on circular needle. You will now be working back and forth in body pat st.

ARMHOLE SHAPING
Bind off 5 (6, 7, 7, 8) sts at beg of next 2 rows, 4 sts at beg of next 2 rows, 3 sts at beg of next 2 rows, then 2 sts at beg of next 2 rows.
Dec row (RS) K1, ssk, work to last 3 sts, k2tog, k1. Work next row even. Rep last 2 rows 1 (2,4, 4, 5) times more—94 (102,108,114,122) sts. Work even until armhole measures 7½ (8, 8½, 9, 9½)"/19 (20.5, 21.5, 23, 24)cm, end with a WS row.

SHOULDER SHAPING
Bind off 28 (31, 34, 36, 39) sts at beg of next 2 rows. Place rem 38

(40, 40, 42, 44) sts on holder for back neck.

FRONT
Work same as back until armhole measures 3½ (4, 4½, 5, 5½)"/9 (10, 11.5,12.5,14)cm, end with a WS row.

NECK SHAPING
Next row (RS) Work across first 40 (43, 46, 48, 51) sts, *place next 7 (8, 8, 9, 10) sts on holder; rep from * once more, join a 2nd ball of yarn and work across last 40 (43, 46, 48, 51) sts. Working both sides at once, work next row even. Bind off 4 sts from each neck edge once, 3 sts once, then 2 sts once, end with a WS row. Dec 1 st from each neck edge on next row, then every other row twice more—28 (31, 34, 36, 39) sts each side. Work even until piece measures same length as back to shoulder, end with a WS row. Bind off each side for shoulders.

SLEEVES
With smaller straight needles, cast on 55 (55, 57, 57, 59) sts. Work in k1, p1 rib for 2"/5cm, end with a WS row. Change to larger straight needles and St st. Inc 1 st each side on next row, then every 4th row 0 (0, 0, 1, 7) times more, every 6th row 0 (0, 8, 22, 18) times, every 8th row 2 (17, 11, 0, 0) times, then every 10th row 12 (0, 0, 0, 0) times—85 (91, 97, 105, 111) sts. Work even until piece measures 20"/51cm from beg, end with a WS row.

CAP SHAPING

Bind off 5 (6, 7, 7, 8) sts at beg of next 2 rows, 4 sts at beg of next 2 rows, 3 sts at beg of next 2 rows, then 2 sts at beg of next 2 rows.
Dec row (RS) K1, ssk, knit to last 3 sts, k2tog, k1. Purl next row.
Rep last 2 rows 1 (2, 4, 4, 5) times more. Bind off 2 sts at beg of next 20 (20, 20, 22, 22) rows.
Bind off rem 13 (15, 15, 19, 21) sts.

FINISHING

Block pieces to measurements. Sew shoulder seams.

HOOD

With RS facing and larger circular needle, k 7 (8, 8, 9, 10) sts from second front neck holder, pick up and k 41 sts evenly spaced along right front neck edge, k 38 (40, 40, 42, 44) sts from back neck holder, pick up and k 41 sts evenly spaced along left front neck edge, k 7 (8, 8, 9, 10) sts from first front neck holder—134 (138, 138, 142, 146) sts.
Next row (WS) P 67 (69, 69, 71, 73) sts, pm, p 67 (69, 69, 71, 73) sts.
Cont in St st and work even for 12 (12, 12½, 13, 13)"/30.5 (30.5, 31.5, 33, 33)cm, end with a WS row.
Dec row (RS) Knit to 4 sts before marker, k2tog, k2, sl marker, k2, ssk, knit to end. Purl next row.
Rep last 2 rows 11 times more.
Bind off rem 110 (114, 114, 118, 122) sts. Sew hood seam. Sew sleeve seams. Set in sleeves. ●

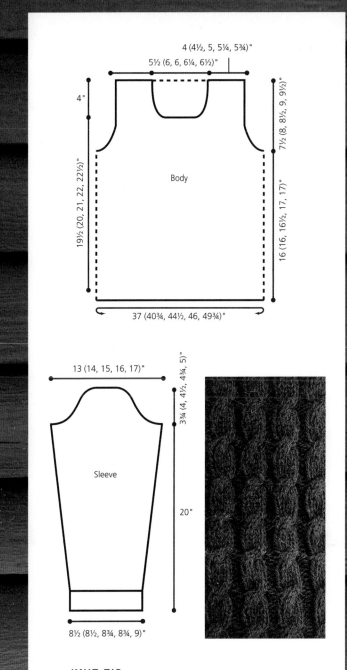

4 (4½, 5, 5¼, 5¾)"

5½ (6, 6, 6¼, 6½)"

4"

Body

7½ (8, 8½, 9, 9½)"

19½ (20, 21, 22, 22½)"

16 (16, 16½, 17, 17)"

37 (40¾, 44½, 46, 49¾)"

13 (14, 15, 16, 17)"

3¾ (4, 4½, 4¾, 5)"

Sleeve

20"

8½ (8½, 8¾, 8¾, 9)"

KNIT TIP

■ Practice knitting cables without a cable needle for a quicker knit!

NORTHEAST

An artisanal approach to yarn

Company Stats

COMPANY STARTED
The Fibre Company, 2003;
Kelbourne Woolens, 2008

PROPRIETORS
The Fibre Company was
founded by Iain Stanley and
Daphne Marinopoulos;
Kelbourne Woolens was
founded by Kate Gagnon
Osborn and Courtney Kelley

LOCATION
Philadelphia, Pennsylvania

YARNS
Seven types, one made in the
United States

BUSINESS PHILOSOPHY
*To develop strong
relationships with
manufacturing
partners and bring an
artisanal approach to
the industry.*

WEBSITE
thefibreco.com,
kelbournewoolens.com

After moving to Maine from England, Iain Stanley and Daphne Marinopoulos began processing fiber for farmers looking to add value to their operations.

After 6 months, they began to experiment with mixing various fibers in small, hand-crafted batches, eventually creating their first yarn, "Pemaquid," and selling it in their retail shop.

Shortly after, they started a small hand-dyeing operation, creating one-of-a-kind artisanal batches of yarns. They created "Terra," their best selling yarn to this day and the yarn that they feel truly represents their creative vision.

Today, they are able to create these artisanal yarns on a larger scale while still working in small batches with the finest quality materials and characteristic painstaking attention to detail. Originally milled and dyed by Daphne and Iain, "Savannah" was recently reintroduced by an American mill, which has been family owned and operated since 1907, and is now distributed by Kate Gagnon Osborn and Courtney Kelley of Kelbourne Woolens. This yarn has enabled The Fibre Company and Kelbourne Woolens to become part of the textile industrial tradition of the eastern United States, specifically in Pennsylvania.

With The Fibre Company and Kelbourne Woolens' roots being in milling yarns and fully understanding the process, they like to partner with the producer, whether it's working with a large mill or a dyer. They like to say, "Whatever we do, whoever we work with, we do it with the knowledge of having done it all on our own."

Quality takes time, and The Fibre Company and Kelbourne Woolens strive to produce only the highest quality yarns with the highest level of craftsmanship.

1. From left to right: Jocelyn Tunney, Kate Gagnon Osborn and Courtney Kelley with their canine clan

2. Soft and beautiful

■ THE FIBRE COMPANY / KELBOURNE WOOLENS

Scandinavian Hat

■■■■

SIZE
Instructions are written for one size.

FINISHED MEASUREMENTS
Head circumference 21"/53.5cm
Depth 9¾"/24.5cm

MATERIALS
■ 1 1¾oz/50g hank (each approx 160yd/146m) of The Fibre Company *Savannah DK* (merino wool/cotton/linen/soya) each in natural (MC) and chambray (CC) ⬛
■ Sizes 2 and 4 (2.75 and 3.5mm) circular needles, 16"/40cm long *or size to obtain gauge*
■ One set (5) size 4 (3.5mm) double-pointed needles (dpns)
■ Stitch marker

GAUGE
25 sts and 28 rnds to 4"/10cm over St st and chart pats using larger circular needle.
Take time to check gauge

NOTE
To work in the rnd, always read charts from right to left.

For this design, Osborn took inspiration from the Setesdal patterns of Norway. Traditional geometric elements are paired with a more modern yarn and subtle color combination to create a cute and wearable hat.

HAT
With smaller circular needle and MC, cast on 120 sts. Join, taking care not to twist sts on needle. Place marker for end of rnd and sl marker every rnd. Work in k2, p2 rib for 2"/5cm.
Next (inc) rnd *K10, M1; rep from * around—132 sts. Change to larger circular needle.

BEG CHART PAT I
Rnd 1 Work 22-st rep 6 times. Cont to foll chart in this way to rnd 33.

CROWN SHAPING
NOTE Change to dpns (dividing sts evenly between 4 needles) when there are too few sts to work with circular needle.

BEG CHART PAT II
Rnd 1 Work 12-st rep 11 times. Cont to foll chart in this way through rnd 7.
Rnd (dec) 8 Work 12-st rep 11 times—121 sts.
Rnd 9 Work 11-st rep 11 times.
Rnd (dec) 10 Work 11-st rep 11

times—110 sts.
Rnd 11 Work 10-st rep 11 times. Cont to foll chart in this way through rnd 22—11 sts.
Next (dec) rnd With MC, 1, [k2tog] 5 times—6 sts.
Cut yarn, leaving a 8"/20.5cm tail and thread through rem sts. Pull tog tightly and secure end. ●

Chart I

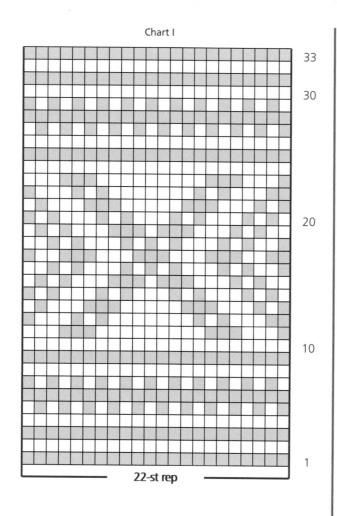

33
30
20
10
1

22-st rep

Chart II

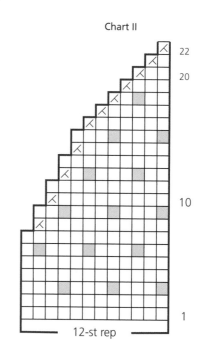

22
20
10
1

12-st rep

Stitch and Color Key

☐ natural (MC)

▨ chambray (CC)

◩ k2tog

■ MORE NORTHEASTERN YARNS
Buy local

ACKER'S ACRES ANGORAS
New Gloucester, Maine
bunnyblend.com

AUTUMN HOUSE FARM
Rochester Mills, Pennsylvania
autumnhousefarm.com

CRANBERRY MOON FARM
Cummington, Massachusetts
goodwool.com

BARTLETTYARNS, INC.
Harmony, Maine
bartlettyarns.com

BEAR MOUNTAIN FARM
West Rupert, Vermont
bearmountainfarm.com

BUCKWHEAT BRIDGE ANGORAS
Elizaville, New York
bwbagoats.com

DECADENT FIBERS
Kinderhook, New York
decadentfibers.com

FORTE FARM
Morris, Connecticut
fortefarm.com

FOXFIRE FIBER DESIGNS
Shelburne, Massachusetts
foxfirefiber.com

GREENWOOD HILL FARM
Hubbardston, Massachusetts
storesonline.com/site/greenwoodhillfarm

HILLTOP HANDSPUN
Lovell, Maine
hilltophandspun.com

HOPE SPINNERY
Hope, Maine
hopespinnery.com

MEADOWCROFT FARM
Washington, Maine
getwool.com

MOONSHINE DESIGN
Colrain, Massachusetts
keldaby.com

MOSTLY MERINO
Putney, Vermont
mostlymerino.com

SCHAEFER YARN
Interlaken, New York
schaeferyarn.com

THIS AND THAT FARM
Putney, Vermont
thisandthatfarm.com

TIDAL YARNS
Old Lyme, Connecticut
tidalyarns.com

THE DESIGNERS

PAM ALLEN is the author of several books including *Knitting for Dummies*. She launched Quince & Co. with her colleagues in July 2010. She lives in Maine.

JOSH BENNETT is a New York City–based knitwear designer. His designs have been published in *Vogue Knitting* and *Knit.1*. He is currently designing and knitting for his website, boymeetspurl.com.

SAUNIELL CONNALLY lives in New York City and works in the fashion industry as a technical designer for knitwear. Her website is sauniellnicole.com/saunshine.

JIL EATON creates two pattern collections annually under her MinnowKnits label, and has just completed her tenth book. Eaton has two yarn lines, which can be seen at minnowknits.com. She lives in Maine.

JARED FLOOD is the owner of Brooklyn Tweed. A photographer and knitwear designer, his designs have been featured in numerous print and online publications.

CORALIE MESLIN picked up needles for the first time six years ago and is now immersed in the craft of knitting, designing and pattern writing. She lives in the San Juan Islands in the Pacific Northwest.

KATE GAGNON OSBORN is the co-owner of Kelbourne Woolens, the distributor of The Fibre Company yarns. She designs regularly for *Interweave Knits* and *Vogue Knitting*.

KAREN JOAN RAZ designs for various yarn companies and publications such as *Vogue Knitting* and *Knitter's*. She lives in Illinois.

CHAPTER 2

South

SOUTH

Shepherds tending their flock

Company Stats

COMPANY STARTED
1993, with yarn manufacturing starting in 2001

PROPRIETORS
Gretchen Frederick and Sue Bundy

LOCATION
Loudoun County, Virginia

YARNS
Fourteen types, all made in the United States

BUSINESS PHILOSOPHY

Motivated by a love of wool and sheep, to support other small farms by creating a market for their good fleeces.

WEBSITE
solitudewool.com

Solitude Wool is owned and operated by Gretchen Frederick and Sue Bundy, two Virginian shepherds who love wool. Both are hand spinners who are taking what they've learned creating yarn from their own flocks and expanding it to create a range of special yarns from other sheep raised locally. They pay fair fleece prices to other small farms in the Chesapeake region, doing their part to help support their local economy.

They also work hard to make the most of the characteristics of each of their neighbors' ten breeds. Each fleece that goes into Solitude Wool yarn is hand-selected at the farm. Different breeds of sheep grow different types of wool—from soft, fine wool, to medium and down type, to lustrous long wool and coarse braid wool.

Keeping the batches small and breed-specific results in yarns that exemplify the character of the fleece.

While Gretchen and Sue feel that the natural color of the yarn coming directly off the sheep is truly the most beautiful, they say they cannot resist hand-dyeing some of the yarn. In fact, it is the color of Solitude Wool yarn that distinguishes it, especially with Gretchen's background in fine art and graphic design. Solitude Wool treats dyeing as art with each lot inspired but not controlled; therefore no dye lots are repeated in their solid, hand-painted variegated or nature dyed yarns.

Keeping their yarns in small batches makes Gretchen and Sue true farm artisans. They feel their yarn is an agricultural product shaped from their combined experiences. They enjoy selling their product at the local farmer's market and relish the opportunity to educate knitters about the different fibers and life on the farm.

1. Taking a stroll
2. Partners in crime
3. From sheep to skein
4. Nature's dye

■ SOLITUDE WOOL

Farmhouse Gloves

■■■■

SIZE
Instructions are written for one size.

FINISHED MEASUREMENTS
HAND CIRCUMFERENCE 7"/18cm
LENGTH OF CUFF approx 3"/7.5cm

MATERIALS
■ 1 4.1oz/116g hank (each approx 133yd/121m) of Solitude *Romney* (wool) each in scarlet (A), soft teal (B), limelight (C), violet (D) and honey orange (E)
■ One set (4) each sizes 6 and 7 (4 and 4.5mm) double-pointed needles (dpns) *or size to obtain gauge*
■ Stitch holders
■ Stitch markers

GAUGE
23 sts and 24 rnds to 4"/10cm over cable rib using larger dpns.
Take time to check gauge.

Kristin Nicholas loves color and is not afraid of using it in her designs. She encourages other knitters to have fun with color by starting with small projects like these vivid gloves. The intricate-looking cabled, corrugated rib cuffs are made by taking two-color ribbing and twisting the stockinette stitches. The effect is impressive but actually quite easy to do.

NOTE
To work in the rnd, always read chart from right to left.

STITCH GLOSSARY
2-st RT Skip next st and knit the 2nd st, then knit the skipped st, sl both sts from needle tog.
M1 With the needle tip, lift the strand between the last stitch worked and the next stitch on left-hand needle and knit into back of it. One knit stitch has been added.
Inc 1 Using the color indicated on chart, cast on 1 st using the backward loop method (see page 75).

CORRUGATED CHECKED PATTERN
(multiple of 6 sts)
Rnd 1 (RS) *K3 with B, k3 with C; rep from * around.

Rnds 2, 3 and 4 *K3 with B, p3 with C; rep from * around.
Rnd 5 *K3 with C, k3 with B; rep from * around.
Rnds 6, 7 and 8 *P3 with C, k3 with B; rep from * around.
Rep rnds 1–8 for corrugated checked pat.

CABLED RIB
(multiple of 4 sts)
Rnd (set-up) 1 (RS) *K1 with D, k2 with E, k1 with D; rep from * around.
Rnd 2 *P1 with D, k2 with E, p1 with D; rep from * around.
Rnd 3 Rep rnd 2.
Rnd 4 *P1 with D, 2-st RT with E, p1 with D; rep from * around.
Rnd 5 Rep rnd 2.
Rep rnds 2–5 for cabled rib.

GLOVES (make 2)
CUFF
With smaller dpn and A, cast on 36 sts and divide sts evenly over 3 needles. Join, taking care not to twist sts on needles, pm for beg of rnds. Work around in St st (k every rnd) for 5 rnds. Cut A. Cont in corrugated checked pat and work rnds 1-8 once, then rnds 1–4 once. Cut B and C.
Change to A.
Next (inc) rnd [K9, M1] 4 times—40 sts.
Purl next rnd. Cut A.

HAND
Change to larger dpns.
Cont in cabled rib and work even for 2"/5cm.

BEG THUMB GUSSET CHART
Rnd (inc) 1 Work 20 sts, pm, Inc 1 with D, pm, work to end—41 sts.
Rnd 2 Work to first marker, sl

marker, p1 with D, sl marker, work to end.
Rnd (inc) 3 Work to first marker, sl marker, Inc 1 with D, p1 with D, Inc 1 with D, sl marker, work to end—43 sts.
Rnd 4 Work to first marker, sl marker, with D, p1, k1, p1, sl marker, work to end.
Rnd (inc) 5 Work to first marker, sl marker, p1 with D, Inc 1 with E, k1 with D, Inc 1 with E, p1 with D, sl marker, work to end—45 sts.
Rnd 6 Work to first marker, sl marker, p1 with D, k1 with E, k1 with D, k1 with E, p1 with D, sl marker, work to end. Cont to foll chart in this way to rnd 14—53 sts.
Next rnd Work to first marker, drop marker, place 13 thumb gusset sts on holder, drop 2nd marker, work to end—40 sts. Cont in cabled rib as established until hand measures 5¼"/13.5cm from last rnd of cuff. Cut D and E.
Change to smaller dpns and A.
Next rnd Knit.
Next rnd Purl. Cut A. Place first 20 sts on one holder and last 20 sts on 2nd holder.

THUMB
Place sts from thumb gusset holder on 2 smaller dpns. With RS facing, join A at beg of thumb sts.
Next rnd Knit across thumb sts, then pick up and k 1 st at base of hand—14 sts. Divide sts between 3 dpns, then pm for beg of rnds.
Next rnd Purl. Cut A. Change to B. Work even in St st until thumb measures 1¾"/4.5cm.

SHAPE TOP
Next (dec) rnd [K2tog] 7 times—7 sts. Cut yarn, leaving a 6"/15.5cm tail. Thread tail in tapestry needle, then thread through rem sts. Pull tog tightly and secure end on WS.

PINKIE
Place first 4 sts from first holder and last 4 sts from 2nd holder on 2 smaller dpns. Join B to 2nd dpn, leaving a 10"/25.5cm tail.
Next rnd K across sts, then cast on 1 st—9 sts. Divide sts evenly between 3 dpns. Join and pm for beg of rnds. Cont to work even in St st for 2"/5cm.

SHAPE TOP
Next (dec) rnd [K2tog] 4 times, k1—5 sts. Finish same as thumb.

RING FINGER
Place next 5 sts from first holder to a smaller dpn and next 5 sts from 2nd holder to a 2nd smaller dpn—10 sts. Join C to 2nd dpn, leaving a 10"/25.5cm tail.
Next rnd K5, pick up and k 1 st at base of pinkie, k5, then cast on 1 st—12 sts. Divide sts evenly between 3 dpns. Join and pm for beg of rnds. Cont to work even in St st for 2½"/6.5cm.

SHAPE TOP
Next (dec) rnd [K2tog] 6 times—6 sts. Finish same as thumb.

MIDDLE FINGER

Place next 6 sts from first holder to a smaller dpn and next 6 sts from 2nd holder to a 2nd smaller dpn—12 sts. Join B to 2nd dpn, leaving a 10"/25.5cm tail.

Next rnd K6, pick up and k 1 st at base of ring finger, k6, then cast on 1 st—14 sts. Divide sts evenly between 3 dpns. Join and pm for beg of rnds. Cont to work even in St st for 2¾"/7cm.

SHAPE TOP

Next (dec) rnd [K2tog] 7 times—7 sts. Finish same as thumb.

INDEX FINGER

Divide rem sts from holders evenly on 2 smaller dpns—10 sts. Join C, leaving a 10"/25.5cm tail.

Next rnd K across, then pick up and k 2 sts at base of middle finger—12 sts. Divide sts as evenly between 3 dpns. Join and pm for beg of rnds. Cont to work even in St st for 2¾"/7cm.

SHAPE TOP

Next (dec) rnd [K2tog] 6 times—6 sts. Finish same as thumb.

FINISHING

Use yarn tails to close up holes between fingers. Weave in ends. ●

BACKWARD LOOP CAST-ON

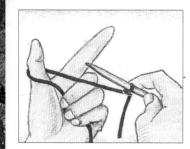

1. Place a slipknot on the right needle, leaving a short tail. Wrap the yarn from the ball around your left thumb from front to back and secure it in your palm with your other fingers.

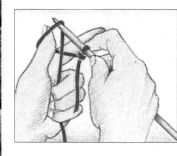

2. Insert the needle upward through the strand on your thumb.

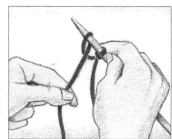

3. Slip this loop from your thumb onto the needle, pulling the yarn from the ball to tighten it. Continue in this way until all the stitches are cast on.

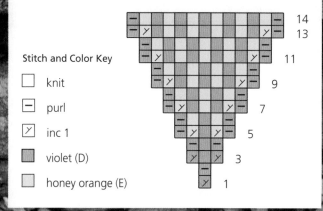

Stitch and Color Key

☐ knit

− purl

⟋ inc 1

▨ violet (D)

☐ honey orange (E)

SOUTH

Quality, innovation, service

Company Stats

COMPANY STARTED
2004

PROPRIETOR
Susan and Mark Moraca

LOCATION
Birmingham, Alabama

YARNS
Thirty-two types, one made in the United States

BUSINESS PHILOSOPHY

To provide the highest-quality products and service in the industry while striving to be the best partners with local yarn shops.

WEBSITE
kollageyarns.com

Kolláge Yarns is a family-owned business run by husband-and-wife team Mark and Susan Moraca. In a continually evolving market and industry, they see an opportunity to provide unique products and offer a wide selection of standard and alternative fibers. They believe that staying in touch with their customers with a willingness to improve their products will further the knitting industry.

They strive to excel in quality control and exceed expectations by providing the best customer support possible and partnering with their local yarn shops.

Seeing their yarns on the cone and in the skein in their offices provides an opportunity for constant monitoring of their product, as well as producing U.S. jobs and supporting the local economy. Their organic "Hope" cotton is milled in the United States, making it one of the few local American cotton yarns. Susan chooses the colors and fibers suitable for each yarn line, getting her inspiration from everything she sees. She names the yarns only after working with them extensively. Always innovative, Kolláge produces several yarns with unusual fibers, such as milk and corn.

The Moracas are proud inventors of circular, double-pointed and single-point square needles and crochet hooks. Made from rosewood and creating more uniform stitches than round ones, the square needles and hooks are easier to hold and enable knitters suffering from carpal tunnel syndrome and arthritis to once again enjoy the craft they love. Promoting chemo cap knitting and blankets for the homeless, they believe in giving back to society and donating as much yarn to charity as possible. Knitting is a passion and that is what they value.

In addition to their thirty-two types of yarn, Kolláge also produces innovative knitting needles and crochet hooks.

■ KOLLÁGE YARNS

Daylily Cardigan

■■■■

SIZE
Instructions are written for Small. Changes for Medium, Large and X-Large are in parentheses.

FINISHED MEASUREMENTS
BUST (buttoned) 32 (36, 40, 44)"/81 (91.5, 101.5, 111.5)cm
LENGTH 15½ (16, 17, 18)"/39.5 (40.5, 43, 45.5)cm
UPPER ARM 12 (13, 14, 15)"/30.5 (33, 35.5, 38)cm

MATERIALS
■ 4 2oz/57g hanks (each approx 160yd/146m) of Kolláge Yarns *Hope USA Cotton DK* (organic cotton) in #6650 natural)
■ One pair size 4 (3.5mm) needles *or size to obtain gauge*
■ Spare size 4 (3.5mm) needle for 3-needle bind-off
■ Stitch holders
■ Stitch markers
■ Five ⅜"/10mm buttons

GAUGE
24 sts and 32 rows to 4"/10cm over lace pat st using size 4 (3.5mm) needles.
Take time to check gauge.

Veronica Parsons likes to borrow from vintage and traditional styles to create garments that are enjoyable to knit and easy to wear. She created this lacy cover-up because she couldn't find the perfect cardi to go over her favorite summer dresses.

SEED STITCH
(over an odd number of sts)
Row 1 (RS) K1, *p1, k1; rep from * to end.
Row 2 K the purl sts and p the knit sts.
Rep row 2 for seed st.

LACE PATTERN STITCH
(multiple of 6 sts plus 1)
Row 1 (RS) K1, *yo, ssk, k1, k2tog, yo, k1; rep from * to end.
Row 2 and all WS rows Purl.
Row 3 K1, *yo, k1, SK2P, k1, yo, k1; rep from * to end.
Row 5 K1, *k2tog, yo, k1, yo, ssk, k1; rep from * to end.
Row 7 K2tog, *[k1, yo] twice, k1, SK2P; rep from * to last 5 sts, end [k1, yo] twice, k1, ssk.
Row 8 Rep row 2.
Rep rows 1–8 for lace pat st.

BACK
Cast on 99 (111, 123, 135) sts.
Work in seed st for 1½"/4cm, end with a RS row.
Purl next row.

Next row (RS) K1 (selvage st), work row 1 of lace pat st to last st, k1 (selvage st).
Next row P1 (selvage st), work row 2 of lace pat st to last st, p1 (selvage st). Keeping 1 st each side in St st for selvage sts, work rem sts in lace pat st and work even until piece measures 8 (8, 8½, 9)"/20.5 (20.5, 21.5, 23)cm from beg, end with a WS row.

ARMHOLE SHAPING
Bind off 4 (5, 6, 7) sts at beg of next 2 rows, then 2 (3, 4, 5) sts at beg of next 2 rows.
Next (dec) row (RS) K1, ssk, work in lace pat st to last 3 sts, k2tog, k1. Work next row even.
Rep last 2 rows 2 (3, 4, 5) times more—81 (87, 93, 99) sts.
Keeping 1 selvage st each side in St st, work even until armhole measures 7½ (8, 8½, 9)"/19 (20.5, 21.5, 23)cm, end with a WS row. Cut yarn.

SHOULDER SHAPING AND BACK NECKBAND
Next row (RS) Place first 23 (25, 28, 30) sts on holder for shoulder, join yarn and work in seed st across center 35 (37, 37, 39) sts for neckband extension, place rem 23 (25, 28, 30) sts on holder for shoulder.

Cont in seed st for 1"/2.5cm, end with a WS row. Bind off in seed st.

LEFT FRONT
Cast on 54 (60, 66, 72) sts.
Next row (RS) *K1, p1; rep from * to end. Beg with row 2, cont in seed st for 1½"/4cm, end with a RS row.
Next row (WS) Work in seed st over first 5 sts (buttonband), pm, purl to end.
Next row (RS) K1 (selvage st), work row 1 of lace pat st to marker, sl marker, work in seed st over last 5 sts.
Next row Work in seed st over first 5 sts, sl marker, work row 2 of lace pat st to last st, p1 (selvage st).
Keeping 1 st at side edge in St st for selvage st and 5 sts at front edge in seed st, work rem sts in lace pat st and work even until piece measures same length as back to underarm, end with a WS row.

ARMHOLE SHAPING
Bind off 4 (5, 6, 7) sts from armhole edge once, then 2 (3, 4, 5) sts once, end with a WS row.
Next (dec) row (RS) K1, ssk, work to end.
Work next row even.
Rep last 2 rows 2 (3, 4, 5) times more—45 (48, 51, 54) sts.

NECK SHAPING
Next (dec) row (RS) Work to 2 sts before marker, k2tog, sl marker, work to end. Rep dec row every other row 9 (10, 10, 11) times more, then every 4th row 7 times—28 (30, 33, 35) sts.
Work even until piece measures same length as back to shoulder, end with a RS row.
Next row (WS) Bind off first 5 sts in seed st, p 23 (25, 28, 30). Place rem 23 (25, 28, 30) sts on holder for shoulder. Place markers for 5 buttons on buttonband, with the first ¾"/2cm from lower edge, the last at beg of neck shaping and the others evenly spaced between.

RIGHT FRONT
Cast on 54 (60, 66, 72) sts.
Next row (RS) *K1, p1; rep from * to end. Beg with row 2, cont in seed st for 1½"/4cm, end with a RS row.
Next row (WS) Purl to last 5 sts, pm, work in seed st over last 5 sts (buttonhole band).
Next row (RS) Work in seed st over first 5 sts, sl marker, work row 1 of lace pat st to last st, end k1 (selvage st).

Next row P1 (selvage st), work row 2 of lace pat st to marker, sl marker, work in seed st over last 5 sts.
Keeping 1 st at side edge in St st for selvage st and 5 sts at front edge in seed st, work rem sts in lace pat st and work even until piece measures same length as back to underarm, end with a RS row. AT THE SAME TIME, work buttonholes opposite markers as foll: Buttonhole row (RS) K1, p1, yo, p2tog, k1, sl marker, work to end.

ARMHOLE SHAPING
Bind off 4 (5, 6, 7) sts from armhole edge once, then 2 (3, 4, 5) sts once, end with a WS row.
Next (dec) row (RS) Work to last 3 sts, k2tog, k1. Work next row even. Rep last 2 rows 2 (3, 4, 5) times more—45 (48, 51, 54) sts.

NECK SHAPING
Next (dec) row (RS) Work in seed st to marker, sl marker, ssk, work to end. Rep dec row every other row 9 (10, 10, 11) times more, then every 4th row 7 times—28 (30, 33, 35) sts. Work even until piece measures same length as back to shoulder, end with a RS row.
Next row (WS) P 23 (25, 28, 30), bind off rem 5 sts in seed st. Place rem 23 (25, 28, 30) sts on holder for shoulder.

SLEEVES
Cast on 81 (87, 93, 99) sts. Work in seed st for 1½"/4cm, end with a RS row. Purl next row.
Next row (RS) K1 (selvage st), work

row 1 of lace pat st to last st, k1
(selvage st).
Next row P1 (selvage st), work row
2 of lace pat st to last st, p1
(selvage st). Keeping 1 st each side
in St st for selvage sts, work rem sts
in lace pat st and work even until
piece measures 2"/5cm from beg,
end with a WS row.

CAP SHAPING
Bind off 4 (5, 6, 7) sts at beg of
next 2 rows, then 2 (3, 4, 5) sts at
beg of next 2 rows.
Dec row 1 (RS) K1, ssk, work in lace
pat st to last 3 sts, k2tog, k1.
Dec row 2 P1, p2tog, work to last
3 sts, p2tog tbl, p1. Rep last 2 rows
once more.
Dec row 3 (RS) K1, ssk, work in lace
pat st to last 3 sts, k2tog, k1.
Work next row even. Rep last 2
rows 15 (16, 17, 18) times more,
then rep dec rows 1 and 2 twice
more. Bind off rem 21 sts.

FINISHING
Block pieces to measurements.
To join left shoulder, place 23 (25,
28, 30) sts from left front holder on
a straight needle ready for a RS row,
then place 23 (25, 28, 30) sts from
left back holder on a straight needle
ready for a RS row. With RS tog,
cont to work 3-needle bind-off. Rep
for right shoulder. Sew bound-off
edges of front neckbands to side
edges of back neckband extension.
Set in sleeves. Sew side and sleeve
seams. Sew on buttons. ●

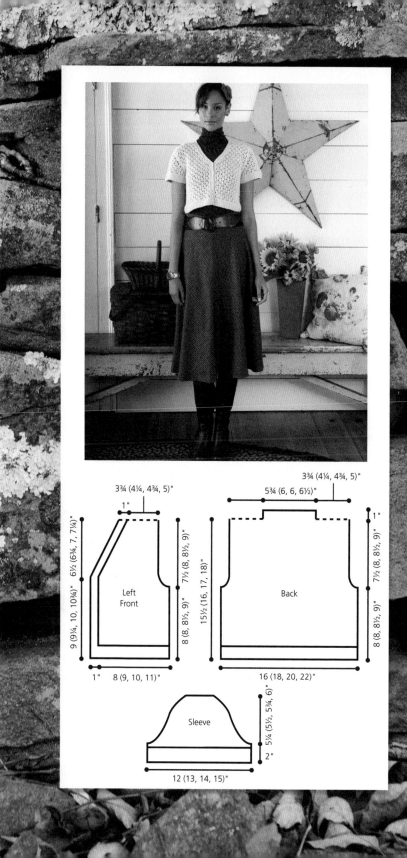

SOUTH

From conception to final product

Company Stats

COMPANY STARTED
2003

PROPRIETORS
Christine and Jeffrey
Charikofsky

LOCATION
Middletown, Maryland

YARNS
Four yarns in multiple weights,
all made in the United States
with limited-edition yarns;
raw fiber, fleece, roving and
sheet felt.

BUSINESS PHILOSOPHY

*To produce U.S.-grown
and milled yarn from
their own alpacas,
providing the
opportunity to improve
raw fiber with each
new generation of
offspring.*

WEBSITE
windsweptalpacas.com

Former software engineers Christine and Jeffrey Charikofsky were looking for a creative diversion and lifestyle change that was non-technology related.

After purchasing land in Maryland, in 1999 and working the local farmers market for a few years selling vegetables, they decided to shift their focus when they lost almost all of their plants in a particularly rainy season. They started raising huacaya alpacas, a relatively new and emerging livestock industry.

Native to South America, the huacaya alpaca, a relative to the camel, produces naturally warm, soft fiber in a multitude of shades. Due to its natural hypoallergenic properties and its lack of "prickle," this fiber can be enjoyed by many people who cannot wear wool. These creatures are intelligent, beautiful and considered eco-friendly because they do not pull up grass from the pasture but actually cut it with their teeth; their manure has very low nitrogen and immediately becomes fertilizer; their soft, padded toes do not gouge the land like hooves; and their fiber does not require the addition of harsh chemicals to remove lanolin

and other contaminants. While alpacas are bred throughout the United States and all over the world, their domestic production remains a specialty market. The U.S. production of alpaca fiber is very low compared to other natural fibers, with only 150,000 registered alpacas.

Alpacas of Windswept Farm is a hands-on operation that breeds its raw fiber source and produces its own unique yarns completely in the United States. Raw fiber from their animals is processed by U.S.–based mills and returned to the farm for hand-dyeing or incorporation into the end product.

In starting their business, this husband-and-wife team had several goals. They wanted to breed high-quality, U.S.-born alpacas for both resale and fiber production in both fleece form and spun yarn and to improve their fleece characteristics with each succeeding generation. They also wanted to maintain an environmentally friendly farm using sustainable agriculture philosophies and blending some of their yarn with bamboo, mohair, wool and silk, which are all sustainable fibers.

1. Sitting pretty
2. Standing tall
3. A captive audience

■ ALPACAS OF WINDSWEPT FARM

Interlocking Rings Cowl

■■■▢

FINISHED MEASUREMENTS
TRUNK RING
NECK CIRCUMFERENCE 20"/51cm
WIDTH 4"/10cm

LEAVES RING
NECK CIRCUMFERENCE
23"/58.5cm
WIDTH 4½"/11.5cm

MATERIALS
■ 1 3.4oz/96g hank (each approx 250yd/229m) of Alpacas of Windswept Farm *100% Alpaca* (alpaca) in rose grey ②
■ Contrasting sock-weight yarn (waste yarn)
■ One pair size 5 (3.75mm) needles *or size to obtain gauge*
■ One size 6 (4mm) circular needle, 16"/40cm long
■ Size F-5 (3.75mm) crochet hook (for chain-st provisional cast-on)
■ Cable needle (cn)
■ Stitch marker

GAUGE
23 sts and 32 rows to 4"/10cm over St st using size 5 (3.75mm) needles. *Take time to check gauge.*

Danielle Romanetti's inspiration for this project came from her love for the environment and her desire to combine complementary stitch patterns in the perfect snuggly cowl. The cabled pattern of the first ring mimics the twisting of tree branches while the open lacework on the second ring brings to mind soft falling leaves. Worked in luxurious and unusually colored alpaca, the finished object is both unique and cozy.

NOTE
To work in the rnd, always read chart from right to left.

STITCH GLOSSARY
20-st RC Sl 10 sts to cn and hold to *back,* k10, k10 from cn.
20-st LC Sl 10 sts to cn and hold to *front,* k10, k10 from cn.

BARK CABLE PATTERN
(over 52 sts)
Row 1 (RS) K9, 20-st RC, k23.
Rows 2, 4 and 6 Purl.
Rows 3 and 5 Knit.
Row 7 K32, 20-st RC.
Rows 8, 10, 12 and 14 Purl.
Rows 9, 11 and 13 Knit.
Row 15 K23, 20-st LC, k9.
Rows 16 and 18 Purl.
Rows 17 Knit.

Row 19 K4, 20-st RC, k28.
Rows 20 and 22 Purl.
Row 21 Knit.
Row 23 K29, 20-st LC, k3.
Rows 24 and 26 Purl.
Rows 25 and 27 Knit.
Row 28 Purl.
Rep rows 1–28 for bark cable pat.

TWISTED BRANCHES RING
With crochet hook and waste yarn, ch 59 for chain-st provisional cast-on. Cut yarn and draw end though lp on hook. Turn ch so bottom lps are at top and cut end is at left. With straight needles, beg 2 lps from right end, pick up and k 1 st in each of next 52 lps. Purl one row, knit one row, purl one row. Cont in bark cable pat and rep rows 1–28 five times.
Leave sts on needle.

FINISHING
Block piece to measurements. With RS facing, release cut end from lp of waste yarn ch. Pulling out 1 ch at a time, place live sts from cast on to a needle. Graft first row of sts to last row of sts using Kitchener stitch (see page 139).

Falling leaves ring

Twisted branches ring

FALLING LEAVES RING

With circular needle, loosely cast on 128 sts. To connect this ring to trunk ring, insert needle through trunk ring, then join, taking care not to twist sts on needle. Place marker for end of rnd and sl marker every rnd. Work around in garter st (knit one rnd, purl one rnd) for 4 rnds.

BEG CHART PAT

Rnd 1 Work 16-st rep 8 times. Cont to foll chart in this way to rnd 16, then rep rnds 1–16 once more. Beg with a purl rnd, work in garter st for 4 rnds. Bind off loosely knitwise. ●

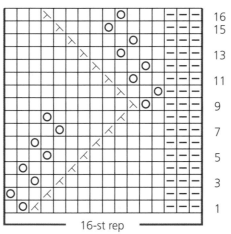

16-st rep

Stitch Key

☐	knit
⊟	purl
⊠	k2tog
⊠	ssk
⊙	yo

An entrepreneurial spirit

Company Stats

COMPANY STARTED
1946

PROPRIETOR
Francis Chester

LOCATION
Churchville, Virginia

YARNS
Eleven types, all except one made in the United States

BUSINESS PHILOSOPHY

To produce yarns made from American-grown cotton and wool and spun on traditional equipment.

WEBSITE
cestariltd.com

In 1946, when he was 10 years old, Francis Chester began his farming career with a vegetable garden in Huntington, New York.

Adding goats and chickens to his repertoire, he honed his business skills by door-to-door marketing and selling his wares at the local farmer's market. As an adult, Chester became interested in sheep, and, after moving to Virginia, he and his wife, Diane, founded two farms, three companies and a complete commercial woolen mill. Cestari has developed its flocks to produce fine Columbia sheep wool and merino wool.

The yarn is spun from American-raised cotton and wool on traditional equipment and is sold throughout the U.S., Australia, Brazil and Canada. Chemical free and ideal for hand-knitting, Cestari's yarns are durable yet soft to the touch and become softer with each successive washing.

1. The wool barn
2. Francis Chester
3. Traditional equipment in a modern world

■ CESTARI

Jennifer Vest

■■■■▶

SIZES
Instructions are written for Small. Changes for Medium, Large, 1X and 2X are in parentheses.

FINISHED MEASUREMENTS
BUST (closed) 34 (37, 41, 45, 49)"/86.5 (94, 104, 114.5, 124.5)cm
LENGTH 21 (21½, 22½, 23½, 24)"/53.5 (54.5, 57, 59.5, 61)cm

MATERIALS
■ 3 (4,4,5,5) 3½oz/100g hanks (each approx 254yd/232m) of Cestari *DK* (cotton/wool) in #179255 lilac heather ❸
■ Size 7 (4.5mm) circular needle, 36"/91cm long *or size to obtain gauge*
■ Size 6 (4mm) circular needles, 16"/41cm and 36"/91cm long
■ One pair size 7 (4.5mm) needles
■ Stitch holders
■ Stitch markers

GAUGE
18 sts and 30 rows to 4"/10cm over St st using larger circular needle. *Take time to check gauge.*

NOTE
Body is made in one piece to underarms.

Connie Chang Chinchio constructed a simple shape with whimsy. The curved hems and ruffles add femininity.

STITCH GLOSSARY
kf&b Inc 1 by knitting into the front and back of the next st.

BODY
With larger circular needle, cast on 88 (104, 120, 140, 156) sts. Work in St st for 2 rows. Shape front edges as foll: using the cable cast-on method, cast on 5 sts at beg of next 2 rows, 4 sts at beg of next 2 rows, 3 sts at beg of next 4 rows, then 2 sts at beg of next 2 rows—122 (138, 154, 174, 190) sts. Cont to shape front edges and set up for dart markers as foll:
Next row (RS) Cast on 2 sts, knit until there are 17 (20, 23, 27, 30) sts on needle, pm, k 16 (18, 20, 22, 24), pm, k 60 (66, 72, 80, 86), pm, k 16 (18, 20, 22, 24), pm, k 15 (18, 21, 25, 28).
Next row Cast on 2 sts, purl to end slipping markers—126 (142, 158, 178, 194) sts. Cont to shape front edges as foll:
Inc row 1 (RS) K1, M1, knit to last st, M1, k1.
Inc row 2 P1, M1 p-st, purl to last st, M1 p-st, p1. Rep last 2 rows once more. Rep Inc row 1 on next row, then every other row 5 times more, then every 4th row 3 times. AT THE

SAME TIME, when piece measures 3 (3, 3½, 4, 4)"/7.5 (7.5, 9, 10, 10)cm from beg (measured from back bottom edge), end with a WS row.

WAIST SHAPING
Next (dec) row (RS) *Work to next marker, sl marker, k2tog, work to 2 sts before next marker, ssk, sl marker; rep from * once more, work to end. Rep this row every 6th row 3 times more. Work until piece measures 7½ (7½, 8, 8½, 8½)"/19 (19, 20.5, 21.5, 21.5)cm from beg, end with a WS row.
Next (inc) row (RS) *Work to next marker, sl marker, M1, work to next marker, M1, sl marker; rep from * once more, work to end. Rep this row every 8th row 3 times more. Work even on 152 (168, 184, 204, 220) sts until piece measures 13½ (13½, 14, 14½, 14½)"/34 (34, 35.5, 37, 37)cm from beg (dropping markers on last row), end with a WS row.

DIVIDE FOR FRONTS AND BACK
Next row (RS) K 34 (37, 40, 44, 47) sts, place sts on holder for right front, bind off next 8 (10, 12, 14, 16) sts for right underarm, work until there are 68 (74, 80, 88, 94) sts on needle for back, bind off next 8 (10, 12, 14, 16) sts for left underarm, work to end; place last 34 (37, 40, 44, 47) sts on holder for left front. *Do not cut yarn.*

BACK

Change to straight needles.
Next row (WS) Rejoin yarn, purl to end—68 (74, 80, 88, 94) sts.

ARMHOLE SHAPING

Dec row (RS) K1, ssk, knit to last 3 sts, k2tog, k1. Purl next row. Rep last 2 rows 4 (5, 6, 7, 8) times more—58 (62, 66, 72, 76) sts. Work even until armhole measures 7 (7½, 8, 8½, 9)"/17.5 (19, 20.5, 21.5, 23)cm, end with a WS row.

NECK SHAPING

Next row (RS) K 15 (17, 18, 20, 22) sts, join a 2nd ball of yarn and bind off center 28 (28, 30, 32, 32) sts, knit to end. Working both sides at once, purl next row. Dec 1 st from each neck edge on next row. Work even on 14 (16, 17, 19, 21) sts each side until armhole measures 7½ (8, 8½, 9, 9½)"/19 (20.5, 21.5, 23, 24)cm, end with a WS row. Place 14 (16, 17, 19, 21) sts each side on holders for shoulders.

LEFT FRONT

Place 34 (37, 40, 44, 47) sts from left front holder on straight needles ready for a WS row. Purl next row.

ARMHOLE AND NECK SHAPING

Dec row (RS) K1, ssk, knit to end. Purl next row. Rep last 2 rows 4 (5, 6, 7, 8) times more. AT THE SAME TIME, when armhole measures 1"/2.5cm, end with a WS row. Shape neck as foll:
Dec row (RS) Work to last 4 sts, k2tog, k2. Purl next row. Rep last 2 rows 14 (14, 15, 16, 16) times. When all shaping has been

completed, work even on 14 (16, 17, 19, 21) sts until piece measures same length at back to shoulder, end with a WS row. Place 14 (16, 17, 19, 21) sts on holder for shoulder.

RIGHT FRONT

Place 34 (37, 40, 44, 47) sts from right front holder on straight needles ready for a WS row. Rejoin yarn. Purl next row.

ARMHOLE AND NECK SHAPING

Dec row (RS) Knit to last 3 sts, k2tog, k1. Purl next row. Rep last 2 rows 4 (5, 6, 7, 8) times more. AT THE SAME TIME, when armhole measures 1"/2.5cm, end with a WS row. Shape neck as foll:
Dec row (RS) K2, ssk, work to end. Purl next row. Rep last 2 rows 14 (14, 15, 16, 16) times more. When all shaping has been completed, work even on 14 (16, 17, 19, 21) sts until piece measures same length at back to shoulder, end with a WS row. Place 14 (16, 17, 19, 21) sts on holder for shoulder.

FINISHING

Block piece to measurements. To join left shoulder, place 14 (15, 17, 19, 21) sts from left front holder on a straight needle ready for a RS row, then place 14 (15, 17, 19, 21) sts from left back holder on a straight needle ready for a RS row. With WS tog, cont to work 3-needle bind-off (seam will be on the RS; as shown). Rep for right shoulder.

OUTER RUFFLE

With RS facing and longer, smaller circular needle, beg at left shoulder

seam and pick up and k 30 (32, 34, 36, 38) sts evenly spaced along left front neck edge, 36 (36, 38, 40, 40) sts along straight front edge, 36 sts along curved edge, 76 (83, 92, 102, 110) sts along back bottom edge, 36 sts along curved edge, 36 (36, 38, 40, 40) sts along straight front edge, 30 (32, 34, 36, 38) sts along right front neck edge, then 34 (34, 36, 38, 38) sts along back neck edge—314 (325, 344, 364, 376) sts. Join and pm for beg of rnds.
Next (inc) rnd *Kf&b; rep from * around—628 (650, 688, 728, 752) sts. Knit next 5 (5, 6, 8, 8) rnds. Bind off all sts loosely purlwise.

ARMHOLE RUFFLE

With RS facing and shorter circular needle, skip first 4 (5, 6, 7, 8) sts of underarm bind-off, pick up and k 78 (84, 90, 96, 102) sts evenly spaced around entire armhole edge. Join and pm for beg of rnds.
Next (inc) rnd *Kf&b; rep from * around—156 (168, 180, 192, 204) sts. Knit next 5 (5, 6, 8, 8) rnds. Bind off all sts loosely purlwise. ●

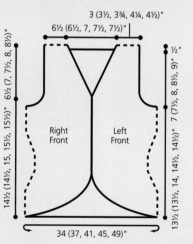

3 (3½, 3¾, 4¼, 4½)"

6½ (6½, 7, 7½, 7½)"

6½ (7, 7½, 8, 8½)"

½"

Right Front

Left Front

14½ (14½, 15, 15½, 15½)"

13½ (13½, 14, 14½, 14½)"

7 (7½, 8, 8½, 9)"

34 (37, 41, 45, 49)"

Striking gold

Company Stats

COMPANY STARTED
2004

PROPRIETORS
Cecil, Ron and Theresa
Miskin

LOCATION
Burleson, Texas

YARNS
Six different yarns, all
incorporating American
bison fiber

BUSINESS PHILOSOPHY
*Striving for perfection,
one project at a time.*

WEBSITE
buffalogold.net

Cecil Miskin has been raising bison, also known as buffalo, since 1991 and working seriously with bison fiber since 1998. In 2004, he sold a box with three pounds of shed buffalo fluff on eBay for $420. The winner wasn't sure what to do with it and sent it back, where it was given to master spinner Elizabeth Lang and planted the idea for a yarn line. Buffalo Gold started with the production of roving and bison down. Having been raising bison for over ten years by the time, Miskin discovered there was both use and value to the soft brown fluff bison shed each year. Buffalo Gold began developing yarns, which quickly grew into a coveted luxury brand.

In 2008, Buffalo Gold launched "Herdwear," its own line of bison fiber accessories, hats, socks, and the very successful "One World" gloves. In 2009, after surviving 4 years with only one color of yarn—brown—Buffalo Gold introduced a new blended yarn, "Lux": a bison, cashmere, silk, and Dupont Tencel creation, in 15 colors. They started a series of collaborations with world-class dyers, making these limited-edition yarns some of the most popular Buffalo Gold yarns ever.

1. Watchful
mom and calf
2. Baby bison

SOUTH

SOUTH

■ BUFFALO GOLD

Wildflowers Scarf

■■■□

FINISHED MEASUREMENTS
Approx 4½" x 74"/11.5cm
x 188cm

MATERIALS
■ 1 1.4oz/40g skein
(approx 320yd/302m) of Buffalo
Gold *Lux* (American bison
downs/cashmere/silk/Tencel)
in pine ①

■ Size E/4 (3.5mm) crochet hook *or
size to obtain gauge*

GAUGE
18 sts to 4"/10cm over dc using
size E-4 (3.5mm) crochet hook.
Take time to check gauge.

NOTE
Scarf is crocheted horizontally
from one long side edge to
opposite long side edge.

STITCH GLOSSARY
dc2tog [Yo, insert hook in next dc,
yo and draw up a lp, yo,
draw through 2 lps on hook]
twice, yo and draw through all
3 lps on hook.

Colorful bunches of wildflowers
are sure markers of spring in the
Texas Hill Country. Blooming
bluebonnets, wine cups and
Indian paintbrushes dance along
the sides of highways and in
nearly every available green
space. From the car, their colors
blur on green grass, but up close
you can see the intricacy of each
petal. This luxurious scarf was
inspired by these simple flowers,
the shapes of which you can
only see upon close examination
of the scarf.

SCARF
Row 1 (RS) Dc in 3rd ch from hook
(first 3 ch skipped counts as 1 dc),
dc in each ch across—340 dc. Turn.
Row 2 Ch 3 (always counts as 1 dc),
dc in next 2 dc, *2 dc in next st, ch
1, sk 2 dc, dc in next dc, ch 1,
sk 2 dc, 2 dc in next dc, dc in next
dc; rep from * across, end dc in last
st—84 ch-1 sps. Turn.
Row 3 Ch 3, dc in next 2 dc,
*dc2tog over next 2 dc, ch 2,
sk 1 dc, dc in next dc, ch 2, sk 1 dc,
dc2tog over next 2 dc, dc in next
dc; rep from * across, end dc in last
2 dc—84 ch-2 sps. Turn.
Row 4 Ch 3, dc in each st across—
336 dc. Turn.
Row 5 Rep row 4.
Row 6 Ch 3, dc in next dc, *2 dc in
next dc, ch 1, sk 2 dc, dc in next dc,
ch 1, sk 2 dc, 2 dc in next dc;

rep from * across, end dc in last 2
dc—96 ch-1 sps. Turn.
Row 7 Ch 3, dc in next dc, *dc2tog
over next 2 dc, ch 2, sk 1 dc, dc in
next dc, ch 2, sk 1 dc, dc2tog over
next 2 dc; rep from * across, end dc
in last 2 dc—96 ch-2 sps. Turn.
Rows 8 and 9 Rep row 4.
Rows 10 and 11 Rep rows 2 and 3.
Row 12 Rep row 4. Fasten off.

FINISHING
Lightly block to finished
measurements. ●

Where the animals come first

Company Stats

COMPANY STARTED
2007

PROPRIETOR
Susan Gibbs

LOCATION
Palmyra, Virginia

YARNS
Four weights of yarn, combed Cormo top, roving and natural-dyed mohair locks, all made in the United States

BUSINESS PHILOSOPHY

That a healthy, contented flock produces superior yarn customers can feel good about knitting with.

WEBSITE
junipermoonfarm.com

At Juniper Moon Farm there is one rule: The animals eat first. That means that owner Susan Gibbs doesn't sit down to a meal until after the flock does—or sometimes not at all!

Home to a flock of registered Cormo sheep and angora goats, Juniper Moon Farm regularly micron-tests the animals' fiber and breeds them for fine fleeces and good mothering abilities. It is a no-kill farm that raises animals for fiber rather than food, which means that the animals sometimes live into their teens, something almost unheard of in today's farming practices. The motto of Juniper Moon Farm is "We believe that an animal that has given us fleece and lambs deserves the happiest life we can provide for them."

Dedicated to producing the finest fleeces, roving and yarn by giving the animals the best possible care means having a deep level of commitment and raising them on a natural diet of pasture and hay. After the fleece is processed by a small, family-owned mill, the yarn is then returned to the farm in its natural state for hand-dyeing. New colorways are introduced quarterly, and naming the colorways and dyeing the yarn is one of Gibbs's favorite parts of owning a fiber farm.

The originator of the Yarn and Fiber CSA (Community Supported Agriculture), Juniper Moon Farm sells advance shares of the spring shearing harvest to knitters and spinners looking for a deeper connection to their fiber. Knitters are able follow the progress of the flock over the course of a year on the farm blog and LambCam, a live video feed starring the lambs. Each month, Juniper Moon Farm holds Open Farm Day for the customers to meet the flock and help name the lambs in the spring; in addition, there are two large shearing parties held each year.

JUNIPER MOON
FARM
JUNIPERMOON.COM

Yarn Shop is Open

1. Open for business
2. The dyeing barn
3. Lambing season
4. Protector of the flock
5. Owner Susan Gibbs

JUNIPER MOON FARM

McEnroe Diamonds Scarf

■■■■

FINISHED MEASUREMENTS
Approx 5" x 53"/12.5cm x 134.5cm

MATERIALS
■ 2 3.5oz/100g hanks (each approx 300yd/274m) of Juniper Moon Farm *Fine Wool Worsted Weight* (domestic fine wool) in farm fresh butter **(4)**
■ One pair size 5 (3.75mm) needles *or size to obtain gauge*
■ Two cable needles (cn)
■ Stitch markers

GAUGE
28 sts and 32 rows to 4"/10cm over chart pats using size 5 (3.75mm) needles.
Take time to check gauge.

Being adopted by an Irish family, Ben Walker was raised with an affinity for cables. Learning that they could be reversible (seen on both sides of the garment), he decided to experiment. The result is a striking diamond cable. This classic neck warmer can be worn without having to worry if the "right" side of the fabric is being flaunted.

STITCH GLOSSARY
8-st LC Sl 4 sts to cn and hold to *front*, [k1, p1] twice, [k1, p1] twice from cn.
8-st RC Sl 4 sts to cn and hold to *back*, [k1, p1] twice, [k1, p1] twice from cn.
5-st DCRP Sl 1 st to cn, [hold cn to *back*, k1, hold cn to *front*, p1] twice, p1 from cn.
5-st DCLK On first cn, sl knit sts (1st and 3rd sts) and hold to *front;* on second cn, sl purl sts (2nd and 4th sts) and hold to *back;* k1; [k1 from front cn, p1 from back cn] twice.
5-st DCRK Sl 1 st to cn, [hold cn to *back,* k1, hold cn to *front,* p1] twice, k1 from cn.
5-st DCLP On first cn, sl knit sts (1st and 3rd sts) and hold to *front;* on second cn, sl purl sts (2nd and 4th sts) and hold to *back;* p1; [k1 from front cn, p1 from back cn] twice.

SCARF
Cast on 48 sts. Work in garter st (knit every row) for 6 rows.

SET-UP ROWS BEFORE CHART PATS
Row 1 (RS) K4, *k1, p1; rep from * to last 4 sts, k4.
Row 2 K4, [k1, p1] 4 times, [p1, k1] 4 times, [k1, p1] 4 times, [p1, k1] 4 times, [k1, p1] 4 times, k4.
Row 3 Rep row 1.
Row 4 K4, pm, [k1, p1] 4 times, pm, [p1, k1] 4 times, [k1, p1] 4 times, [p1, k1] 4 times, pm, [k1, p1] 4 times, pm, k4.

BEG CHART PATS
Row 1 (RS) K4, sl marker, work chart I over next 8 sts, sl marker, work chart II over center 24 sts, sl marker, work chart III over next 8 sts, sl marker, k4. Keeping 4 sts each side in garter st, cont to foll charts this way, working charts I and II to row 8, then rep rows 1–8, and working chart III to row 42, then rep rows 1–42 nine times more, then rows 1–10 once.

SET-UP ROWS AFTER CHART PATS
Removing markers on first row, cont as foll: **Row 1** K4, *k1, p1; rep from * to last 4 sts, end k4.
Row 2 K4, [k1, p1] 4 times, [p1, k1] 4 times, [k1, p1] 4 times, [p1, k1] 4 times, [k1, p1] 4 times, k4.
Row 3 Rep row 1. **Row 4** Rep row 2. Work in garter st for 6 rows. Bind off knitwise.

FINISHING
Block piece to finished measurements. ●

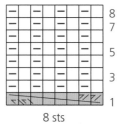

SOUTH

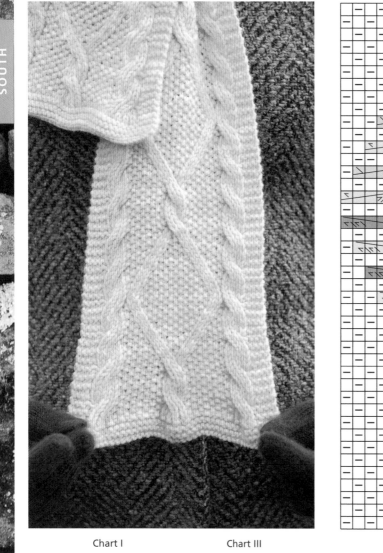

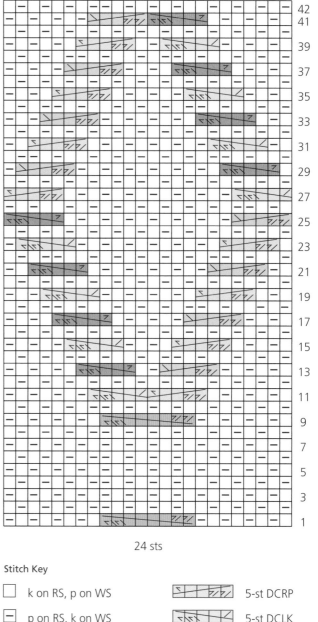

Chart II

42
41
39
37
35
33
31
29
27
25
23
21
19
17
15
13
11
9
7
5
3
1

24 sts

Chart I

8
7
5
3
1

8 sts

Chart III

8
7
5
3
1

8 sts

Stitch Key

☐ k on RS, p on WS

☐ p on RS, k on WS

⬛ 8-st RC

⬛ 8-st LC

5-st DCRP

5-st DCLK

5-st DCRK

5-st DCLP

■ MORE SOUTHERN YARNS

Buy local

4 LAZY J RANCH
Okmulgee County, Oklahoma
4lazyjranch.com

FLAGGY MEADOW FIBER WORKS
Springfield, Kentucky
shop.flaggymeadowfiberworks.com

KAI RANCH
Lexington, Texas
kairanch.com

KID HOLLOW FARM
Free Union, Virginia
kidhollow.com

NEIGHBORHOOD FIBER COMPANY
Baltimore, Maryland
neighborhoodfiberco.com

PISGAH YARN AND DYEING COMPANY
Old Fort, North Carolina
elmore-pisgah.com

THE DESIGNERS

CONNIE CHANG CHINCHIO started out in theoretical condensed matter physics and somehow found her passion in hand-knit design. She currently works in financial services between sweaters and pontificates about knitting, designing and everything in between at conniechangchinchio.com.blog. She lives in New Jersey.

KRISTIN NICHOLAS is an artist and designer who lives in the hills of western Massachusetts on a working sheep farm. She is the author of eight books on knitting and stitching, including *Color by Kristin,* and appears regularly on the PBS show *Knit and Crochet Now.* Her colorful farmhouse, which she shares with her husband and daughter, has been featured in *Country Home* and on Martha Stewart Living TV. She writes the popular blog "Getting Stitched on the Farm" at kristinnicholas.com.

VERONICA PARSONS grew up in Naperville, Illinois and was taught to knit as a child by her mother. Currently living in California, she can be found—when not knitting—in her kitchen whipping up something delicious, puzzling through an endless stack of crosswords or blogging at golden-iris.blogspot.com.

LINDA PERMANN is a crochet designer, writer and local yarn shop junkie. She is the author of *Crochet Adorned* and *Little Crochet* and is a frequent contributor to several crochet and craft magazines. Read more about her crafty adventures at lindamade.com. She lives in Texas.

DANIELLE ROMANETTI learned to knit as a child from her grandmother and made a Cabbage Patch doll scarf as her first project. Moving to the Washington, DC, area from Pittsburgh, she began teaching at a local shop and in 2006 opened Knit-a-Gogo, Inc. Knit-a-Gogo grew, and with the encouragement of the DC area's knitting and crochet community, she opened Fibre Space in July 2009. Read about her shop at fibrespace.com.

BEN WALKER is a born and bred Midwesterner with a love of good food and good fiber. A few years back, a little voice in his head told him to sell all of his video games and related equipment and take up knitting. He hasn't looked back since. He lives in Illinois.

CHAPTER 3

Midwest

Art made by hand

Company Stats

COMPANY STARTED
Started in 1984,
reborn in 2004

PROPRIETORS
Dave and Terri Gentzsch

LOCATION
Jefferson City, Missouri

YARNS
Two types, both made in
the United States

BUSINESS PHILOSOPHY
*To educate the
customer base about
good fiber and how it
feels and looks.*

WEBSITE
ozarkhandspun.com

When visiting their daughter in California after being semi-retired in 2003, Dave and Terri Gentzsch walked into a yarn shop and were disappointed by what they saw.

They had started Ozark Handspun in 1984, but closed it two years later due to the demands of a growing family and an inability to sell outside of the immediate area in the pre-Internet age. Dave knew he could make better yarns than what he saw on sale at that shop, and prompted by a "prove it" response by his wife, went home and restarted Ozark Handspun.

Dave called a friend from 20 years before to locate raw wool and mohair. He brought his old spinning wheel and other equipment out of storage and reacquainted himself with washing, dyeing, carding and spinning. He updated his technology and soon had orders coming in.

Ozark gathers fiber from local farms, therefore creating work for their neighbors and keeping everything local. They minimize processing, which gives their hand-made yarns interesting texture and fiber combinations. Using environmentally friendly dyes and 100-percent hand processing, as well as slow shipping, Ozark considers itself a "green" company and does everything it can to be more so.

People are drawn to this yarn because of the unusual textures and color combinations. Minimal processing means that occasionally small bits of nature will be found in the wool.

Each year as sheep and goats age, their coats change colors. Due to this fact and the unique combination of dyed wools conjured up by Dave's artistic side, Ozark Handspun's yarn is truly a work of art in itself.

1. Dave Gentzsch processing fleece
2. Fleece ready to be made into yarn
3. Secret recipe book
4. All in a day's work

■ OZARK HANDSPUN

Appalachian Hat

■■□□

SIZE
Instructions are written for one size.

FINISHED MEASUREMENTS
HEAD CIRCUMFERENCE
18"/45.5cm (stretches to
21"/53.5cm)
DEPTH 7"/18cm

MATERIALS
■ 1 3½oz/100g hank (each approx
50yd/46m) of Ozark Handspun
Opulent II (mohair/wool) in
#2387DS blue moon (6)
■ One size 15 (10mm) circular
needle, 16"/40cm long *or size to
obtain gauge*
■ One set (5) size 15 (10mm)
double-pointed needles (dpns)
■ Stitch marker
■ 2"/5cm pompom maker
(optional)

GAUGE
8 sts and 13 rnds to 4"/10cm
over St st using size 15 (10mm)
circular needle.
Take time to check gauge.

Growing up in New England, my
parents taught me to appreciate the
beauty of the great outdoors, and
we often went on hikes that were
part of the Appalachian Trail.
Spanning from Georgia to Maine,
this trail covers many of the states
we visited while growing up.
The rustic yarn brings to mind the
warm woolies I'd wear while winter
hiking with my dad and brother.

HAT
With circular needle, cast on 36 sts.
Join, taking care not to twist sts on
needle. Place marker for end of rnd
and sl marker every rnd.
Work in rev St st (purl every rnd) for
2"/5cm. Cont in St st (k every rnd)
until piece measures 5"/12.5cm
from beg.

CROWN SHAPING
NOTE Change to dpns (dividing sts
evenly between 4 needles) when
there are too few sts to work with
circular needle.
Dec rnd 1 *K2tog; rep from *
around—18 sts.
Next rnd Knit.

Rep last 2 rnds once more—9 sts.
Dec rnd 2 [K2tog] 4 times, k1—5
sts. Cut yarn, leaving an 8"/20.5cm
tail and thread through rem sts.
Pull tog tightly and secure end.

POMPOM
Use leftover yarn to make a
2"/5cm pompom using pompom
maker or instructions on page 118.
Sew to top of hat. ●

MIDWEST

Proud to be American

Company Stats

COMPANY STARTED
1980

PROPRIETORS
Harlan and Janet Brown and
Robert and Peggy Jo Wells

LOCATION
Mitchell, Nebraska

YARNS
Fourteen different lines in
various weights, plies
and fibers, all made in the
United States

BUSINESS PHILOSOPHY
*To make quality yarn
by quality people,
offered at economical
prices, with the best
service in the industry.*

WEBSITE
brownsheep.com

The dream of Brown Sheep Company began with Harlan Brown and the purchase of an Ashford spinning wheel. Having worked his grandfather's farm for 35 years and developed an extensive sheep-feeding and wool-production operation, he became convinced he needed to find a way to add value to the product that he already produced and understood—wool.

As a member of the American Sheep Council and the North Central Wool Marketing Association, Brown understood the problems of the American wool market—foremost that the United States growers had continually been plagued with wide market fluctuations in price and demand. In 1980 Harlan and his wife, Janet, purchased spinning equipment, and sixth months later Harlan had his first ball of yarn in his hands. Their first line, "Top of the Lamb," is still going strong to this day. Hitting the road with their new product, they didn't give up when they heard the word "no,"

and soon enough their yarn was making a splash in the Southwest weaving industry and with hand knitters.

By 1982, the Browns' son Robert was learning the fine points of dyeing natural fibers, and soon the original color group grew to fifteen colors. Beginning to experiment with mohair, "Lamb's Pride" was soon born and today continues to be their top seller, with over 70 colors of solid and heathered shades. Continuing to add other fibers over the years, they rounded out the company with an elegant silk blend.

Now run by Harlan and Janet's daughter Peggy Jo Wells and her husband, Robert, Brown Sheep has seen twenty years of steady growth and three years of tremendous increase. This is a testament to a staff that honors their mission statement of offering the best possible product at a good price backed with excellent customer service. Committed to utilizing American-produced fiber for as long as possible, replacing 90 percent of their original spinning equipment with state-of-the-art machinery and using an eco-friendly waste-water system, this family business will continue to grow its reputation for yarns of high quality.

1. Harlan Brown's grandfather, Edward W. Brown, on the family farm, 1910
2. A warm welcome
3. Co-founder Harlan Brown
4. Yarn packaged and ready for market

■ Brown Sheep Company

Random Harvest Afghan

■■■◻

FINISHED MEASUREMENTS
Approx 36" x 54"/91.5cm x 137cm

MATERIALS
■ 2 4oz/113g hanks (each approx 190yd/173m) of Brown Sheep Company *Lamb's Pride Worsted* (wool/mohair) each in #M127 navy sailor (A), #M08 wild oak (B), #M11 white frost (C), #M80 blue blood red (D), #M140 aran (E) and #M116 camel back (F) (④)
■ Size J/10 (6mm) crochet hook *or size to obtain gauge*

GAUGE
One motif is 6½"/16.5cm from point to point and 6"/15cm from side edge to side edge using size J/10 (6mm) crochet hook. *Take time to check gauge.*

NOTE
When changing colors, draw new color through last 2 lps on hook.

Randy Cavaliere designed this orderly, geometric afghan as a response to the fast and chaotic world around her. The circular and hexagon design evokes an era when life was simpler.

STITCH GLOSSARY
FRdc (front raised dc) Yo, working from front to back to front, insert hook around post of stitch of rnd below, yo and draw up a lp, [yo and draw through 2 lps on hook] twice.

AFGHAN
The afghan is made of 7 rows of hexagons that are joined together on the last rnd. Odd rows (1, 3, 5 and 7) have 9 hexagons and even rows (2, 4 and 6) have 8 hexagons. Refer to diagram for color combinations. Make hexagon 1 first, then make hexagon 2 and join hexagon 1 as described on rnd 6 of pat. Working each row from left to right, cont to join hexagons of row 1 as shown on diagram, then proceed to row 2.

HEXAGON 1
With A, ch 5. Join ch with a sl st, forming a ring.
Rnd 1 (RS) Ch 1, work 12 sc in ring, join rnd with a sl st in first sc—12 sc. Turn.
Rnd 2 Ch 4 (counts as first dc and

ch 1), *dc in next st, ch 1; rep from * around, join rnd with a sl st in 3rd ch of beg ch-4—12 dc and 12 ch-1 sps. Turn.
Rnd 3 (RS) Ch 5 (counts as first dc and ch 2), turn, *FRdc around next dc of rnd 2, ch 2, dc in next dc, ch 2; rep from * around, join rnd with a sl st in 3rd ch of beg ch-5—12 dc and 12 ch-2 sps. Turn.
Rnd 4 Sl st in first ch-2 sp, ch 3 (counts as first dc), work 2 dc in same ch-2 sp, ch 1, work (3 dc, ch 2) in next ch-2 sp, *work (3 dc, ch 1) in next ch-2 sp, work (3 dc, ch 2) in next ch-2 sp; rep from * around, join rnd with a sl st in top of beg ch-3 changing to B—36 dc, 6 ch-1 sps and 6 ch-2 sps. Turn.

Placement Diagram

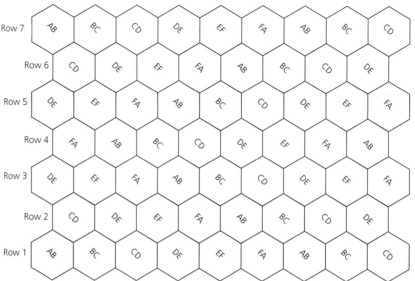

Row 7: AB BC CD DE EF FA AB BC CD
Row 6: CD DE EF FA AB BC CD DE
Row 5: DE EF FA AB BC CD DE EF FA
Row 4: FA AB BC CD DE EF FA AB
Row 3: DE EF FA AB BC CD DE EF FA
Row 2: CD DE EF FA AB BC CD DE
Row 1: AB BC CD DE EF FA AB BC CD

Rnd 5 (RS) Sl st in first ch-2 sp, ch 5 (counts as first tr and ch 1), *skip next dc, FRdc around next dc of rnd 4, ch 1, skip next dc, dc in next ch-1 sp, ch 1, skip next dc, FRdc around next dc of rnd 4, ch 1, skip next dc,** [tr, ch 1] twice in next ch-2 sp; rep from * around ending at **, then work tr in first ch-2 sp, ch 1, join rnd with a sl st in 4th ch of beg ch-5—12 tr, 18 dc and 30 ch-1 sps. Turn.

Rnd 6 Ch 1, sc in first tr, *work (sc, ch 1, sc) in next ch-1 sp (corner sp made), sc in next tr, sc in each ch-1 sp and dc across to next tr**, sc in next tr; rep from * around ending at **, join rnd with a sl st in first sc—66 sc and 6 corner ch-1 sps. Fasten off.

HEXAGON 2
With B, rep rnds 1–5 of hexagon 1, changing to C at end of rnd 4. Turn.

JOINING
Rnd 6 Ch 1, sc in first tr, work (sc, ch 1, sc) in next corner ch-1 sp, sc in next tr, sc in each ch-1 sp and dc across to next tr, sc in next tr and corner ch-1 sp, *with RS tog, join to previously made hexagon with sl st in corner ch-1 sp of rnd 6, sc in same ch-1 sp, sc in next tr, sc in each ch-1 sp and dc across to next tr, sc in next tr and corner ch-1 sp; rep from * as necessary to join to previously made hexagon, sc in same ch-1 sp, **sc in next tr,*** sc in each ch-1 sp and dc across to next tr, sc in next tr, work (sc, ch 1, sc) in next corner ch-1 sp; rep from ** around ending at ***; sc in each ch-1 sp and dc to first sc, join rnd with a sl st in first sc. Fasten off.

FINISHING
Lightly block piece to measurements. ●

■ DREAM IN COLOR

For the love of color

Company Stats

COMPANY STARTED
2006

PROPRIETORS
Veronica Van and
Nancy Leuer

LOCATION
West Chicago, Illinois

YARNS
Superwash merino in various
weights, all spun and dyed in
the United States

BUSINESS PHILOSOPHY

*To dye excellent yarn
at an affordable price
and have fun doing it,
making yarn with joy,
laughter and passion.*

WEBSITE
dreamincoloryarn.com

While owning a local yarn shop, Veronica Van and Nancy Leuer founded Dream in Color to meet their customers' demand for a hand-dyed, easy-to-care-for and affordable yarn. After searching without success, they decided to create it themselves, and "Classy" was born.

A fiber artist by trade, Van developed a new technique for dyeing yarn that would knit up in a totally random fashion with a multitude of hues. Calling it "veil-dyed," they engineered a process so their yarns could be dyed in large batches while maintaining their striking colorways, bringing depth and life to the color, giving it dramatic shimmer and shine with all the unique characteristics of other hand-dyed yarns, but without pooling (when blocks of one color appear in the yarn while being knit up). Each colorway is named after its own personality.

Van and Lauer take great pride in their fiber, which is milled by Kraemer Textiles in Pennsylvania. Their yarn base is a soft and easy-care merino that is machine-washable.

1. Dream in Color
co-owner Veronica Van
2. A range of luminous
colorways

■ DREAM IN COLOR

Sousa's Mitts

■■■□

SIZE
Instructions are written for one size.

FINISHED MEASUREMENTS
HAND CIRCUMFERENCE
7"/17.5cm
LENGTH OF CUFF approx
2½"/6.5cm

MATERIALS
■ 1 4oz/113g hank (each approx 250yd/229m) of Dream in Color *Classy* (superfine merino wool) each in crying dove (MC), night watch (A) and lipstick (B) (4)
■ One set (4) size 8 (5mm) double-pointed needles (dpns) *or size to obtain gauge*
■ Stitch holder
■ Stitch markers

GAUGE
18 sts and 24 rnds to 4"/10cm over St st using size 8 (5mm) dpns. *Take time to check gauge.*

I have a flag obsession that goes back to childhood. Inspired by our country's patriotism that is roused during the Olympics, and living in Washington, DC, with many friends in politics or working for the government, I created these mitts as a way to show my pride in my country with a wave of my hand.

CORRUGATED RIB
(multiple of 2 sts)
Rnd 1 *K1 with MC, p1 with B; rep from * around.
Rep rnd 1 for corrugated rib.

MITTEN (make 2)
CUFF
With A, cast on 30 sts. Divide sts over 3 needles (10 sts on each). Join, taking care not to twist sts on needles, pm for beg of rnd. Cont in corrugated rib for 2½"/6.5cm.
Cut A and B.
Cont in St st with MC only as foll:

HAND
Next (inc) rnd Knit to last st, M1, k1—31 sts.

THUMB GUSSET
Inc rnd 1 K 15, pm, M1, k1, M1, pm, k to end—33 sts. Knit next rnd.
Inc rnd 2 K to first marker, sl marker, M1, k3, M1, sl marker, k to end—35 sts. Knit next 2 rnds.

Inc rnd 3 K to first marker, sl marker, M1, k5, M1, sl marker, k to end—37 sts. Knit next 2 rnds.
Inc rnd 4 K to first marker, sl marker, M1, k7, M1, sl marker, k to end—39 sts. Knit next 2 rnds.
Inc rnd 5 K to first marker, sl marker, M1, k9, M1, sl marker, k to end—41 sts.
Next rnd K to first marker, drop marker, place next 11 sts on st holder, drop marker, cast on 1 st, k to end—31 sts. Cont in St st until piece measures 7½"/19cm from beg.

TOP SHAPING
Dec rnd 1 K1, [k8, k2tog] 3 times—28 sts.
Dec rnd 2 [K5, k2tog] 4 times—24 sts. Knit next rnd.
Dec rnd 3 [K4, k2tog] 4 times—20 sts.
Dec rnd 4 [K3, k2tog] 4 times—16 sts.
Dec rnd 5 [K2, k2tog] 4 times—12 sts.
Dec rnd 6 [K1, k2tog] 4 times—8 sts.
Dec rnd 7 [K2tog] 4 times—4 sts.
Cut yarn, leaving a 6"/15cm tail and thread through rem sts. Pull tog tightly and secure end.

THUMB

Place 11 thumb gusset sts
over 2 needles.

Next rnd Join MC, leaving a long
tail for sewing and knit across sts,
then pick up and k 1 st at base of
hand—12 (13) sts. Divide sts evenly
over 3 needles. Join and pm for beg
of rnds. Cont in St st for 1½"/4cm.

TOP SHAPING

Dec rnd [K2tog] 6 times—6 sts.
Knit next rnd. Cut yarn, leaving a
6"/15cm tail and thread through
rem sts. Pull tog tightly and
secure end.

FINISHING

For each mitten, use MC tail
to sew gap between thumb and
hand closed.

DUPLICATE STITCH EMBROIDERY

Place left mitten flat on work
surface so back is facing you.
Count 19 rnds from end of ribbing
and mark with a pin placed
horizontally. Count in from each
side edge and mark center 10 sts
with pins placed vertically. First row
of duplicate stitch is across the
20th rnd and centered between
vertical pins. Using tapestry needle,
embroider duplicate stitches (see
page 149) foll chart using
A and B as shown. Rep for right
mitten. Block pieces lightly to
measurements. ●

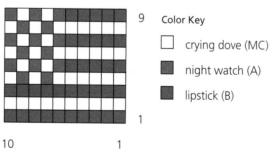

Color Key

☐ crying dove (MC)

■ night watch (A)

■ lipstick (B)

KNIT TIP

■ Saturated hues can bleed on white fiber during blocking.
Use a fan after wet-blocking to prevent bleeds.

■ STONEHEDGE FIBER MILL

All in the family

Company Stats

COMPANY STARTED
1999

PROPRIETOR
Debra McDermott

LOCATION
East Jordan, Michigan

YARNS
Two types in different weights, as well as roving and batts, all made in the United States

BUSINESS PHILOSOPHY

To strive to produce a quality product that is a joy for people to work with.

WEBSITE
stonehedgefibermill.com

Having worked with fiber and fiber animals for over 18 years, Debra McDermott wears many hats as a shepherd, spinner and fiber artist.

Stonehedge Fiber Mill is a family-owned and operated 150-year-old farm that in 1999 added another dimension when it began processing fiber. In addition to its fiber shop and processing mill, Stonehedge produces its own yarn line, the very popular, 100-percent American-made, merino Shepherd's Wool. Shepherd's Wool comes in dozens of colors as well as twisted colorways. It is carried in more than 80 stores across the county with plans for expansion.

McDermott had a goal of processing 500 pounds of yarn per month during Stonehedge's first year as a yarn company. After it became clear the equipment purchased would not be able to keep up with the demand, her husband, Chuck, who had worked at General Motors, was given the task of creating equipment that could. As a result of Chuck's knowledge and skill, Stonehedge now produces 1,500 pounds of yarn per month and offers its own line of yarn-production equipment, including carding machines, pickers and tumblers, spinners, pindrafters, needle felters and skein- and cone-winders used in mills across the country.

1. Spinning yarn
2. Twisted roving ready to become yarn

■ STONEHEDGE FIBER MILL

Picnic Kerchief

■■■▭

SIZE
Instructions are written for child's size.

FINISHED MEASUREMENTS
14½"/37cm wide (excluding ties)
7¼"/18.5cm long

MATERIALS
■ 1 4oz/113g hank (each approx 250yd/229m) of Stonehedge Fiber Mill *Shepherd's Wool* (merino wool) each in garnet (MC) and cherries jubilee (CC) (4)
■ One pair size 7 (4.5mm) needles *or size to obtain gauge*
■ Two size 6 (4mm) double-pointed needles (dpns) (for I-cords)

GAUGE
16 sts and 26 rows to 4"/10cm over St st using 2 strands of MC held tog and size 7 (4.5mm) needles. *Take time to check gauge.*

NOTES
1) Use 2 strands of MC held tog throughout.
2) Use 1 strand of CC throughout.

For Larissa Brown, an inspiring design builds on a basic shape as a canvas for ideas, textures and embellishments. In this case, a simple triangle was the jumping-off point for something playful. The yarn inspired her to keep the design simple and allow its deep and complex tones to sing. The variegated colorway prompted an I-cord edging that flows continuously to become the kerchief's ties.

KERCHIEF
With larger needles and 2 strands of MC held tog, cast on 75 sts.
Row 1 (RS) Ssk, k33, [ssk] twice, k2tog, k32, k2tog—70 sts.
Row 2 Purl.
Row 3 Ssk, knit to 2 sts before first ssk in center of previous RS row, ssk, [k2tog] twice, knit to last 2 sts, k2tog—65 sts.
Row 4 Purl.
Row 5 Ssk, knit to 1 st before first ssk in center of previous RS row, [ssk] twice, k2tog, knit to 2 sts before end, k2tog—60 sts.
Row 6 Purl.
Rep rows 3–6 until 10 sts rem.
Next (dec) row (RS) [Ssk] twice, [k2tog] 3 times—5 sts.
Purl next row.
Next (dec) row (RS) Ssk, k1, k2tog—3 sts. Bind off purlwise.

FINISHING
Block triangle so long edge measures 15"/38cm and side edges measure 10"/25.5cm.

I-CORD SIDE EDGING
Beg and ending at long top edge, edging is worked down one side edge, around bottom point and up opposite side edge. With dpns and 1 strand of CC, cast on 4 sts, leaving a long tail for sewing. Beg attached I-cord over as foll:
Next row (RS) *Slide sts to opposite end of needle, with 2nd dpn, k4. With WS of kerchief facing, use tip of RH needle to pick up and k 1 st in side edge of kerchief, 1 row below top edge—5 sts on RH needle. Cont I-cord as foll:
Next row (RS) *Slide sts to opposite end of needle, with 2nd dpn, k3, k2tog. Pick up and k 1 st in next row along side edge; rep from * around to opposite, ending 1 row below long top edge. Bind off knitwise.

I-CORD TIES AND TOP EDGING
With dpn and 1 strand of CC, cast on 4 sts, leaving a long tail for sewing. Work I-cord as foll: *Next row (RS) With 2nd dpn, k4, do not turn. Slide sts back to beg of needle to work next row from RS; rep from * until I-cord measures 16"/40.5cm from beg. Do not bind off. With WS of kerchief facing, work I-cord edging across long top edge, beg and ending across top edges of I-cord edging. Cont to work opposite tie and work for 16"/40.5cm. Cut yarn, leaving a long tail. Thread tail in tapestry needle and weave through sts. Pull tight to gather, fasten securely.

POMPOMS (MAKE 2)
Using CC, make two 2"/5cm diameter pompoms (see below). Sew pompoms to ends of ties. ●

HOW TO MAKE A CLASSIC AMERICAN POMPOM

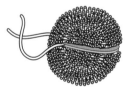

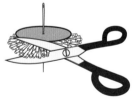

1. Cut a center hole in two circular pieces of cardboard the width of the desired pompom. Then cut a pie-shaped wedge out of each circle.

2. Hold the two circles together and wrap the yarn tightly around the cardboard. Carefully cut around the cardboard.

3. Tie a piece of yarn tightly between the two circles. Remove the cardboard and trim the pompom. Hold the two circles together and wrap the yarn tightly around the cardboard. Then carefully cut around the cardboard.

4. Sandwich the pompom between two round pieces of cardboard held together with a long needle. Cut around the circumference for a perfect pompom.

■ MORE MIDWESTERN YARNS

Buy local

BLACKBERRY RIDGE WOOLEN MILL
Mount Horeb, Wisconsin
blackberry-ridge.com

BRIAR ROSE FIBERS
Michigan
briarrosefibers.net

COLORATURA YARNS
Baltimore, Ohio
coloraturayarns.com

CORNY GOODNESS
Minnesota
cornygoodness.com

DAKOTA CARDING AND WOOL
Groton, South Dakota
dakotacardingandwool.com

GREATWOOL
Minnesota
greatwool.com

HIDDEN VALLEY FARM & WOOLEN MILL
Valders, Wisconsin
hiddenvalleyfarmwoolenmill.com

MARR HAVEN
Allegan, Wisconsin
marrhaven.com

MISTI ALPACA
Glen Ellyn, Illinois
mistialpaca.com

MISTY MEADOWS
Minnetrista, Minnesota
mistymeadowicelandics.com

RIVERWINDS FARM
Boyd, Wisconsin
riverwindsfarm.com

SHEEP STREET FIBERS
Morgantown, Indiana
sheepstreet.com

SERENITY FARMS
Alma, Michigan
serenity-farms.com

THE DESIGNERS

LARISSA BROWN is a designer, yarn dyer and author of the book *Knitalong: Celebrating the Tradition of Knitting Together*. Her work plays on the unexpected, adding a small twist to each knitting design using unusual contrasts in colorways she designs for Pico Accuardi Dyeworks. Larissa just finished her second book, *My Grandmother's Knitting*. Check out her blog at stitchmarker. tumblr.com. She lives in Oregon.

RANDY CAVALIERE, aka The Yarn Princess, is a crochet designer, teacher and technical editor who lives in her native Brooklyn with her husband and countless skeins of yarn. Genetically geared towards handcrafts and fiber arts, she learned to crochet in 2001 after nearly 40 years of sewing and needlework. She is grateful on a daily basis for her husband, Tony, who believes she should have all the yarn her heart desires.

CHAPTER 4

West

A sustainable legacy

Company Stats

COMPANY STARTED
The ranch was established in 1871 and has been producing sheep since 1873. Imperial Yarn started in 1999.

PROPRIETORS
Dan and Jeanne Carver

LOCATION
Maupin, Oregon

YARNS
Ten types in addition to roving, all made in the United States

BUSINESS PHILOSOPHY
To be a socially and environmentally responsible yarn company committed to healthy local economies and balanced business practices.

WEBSITE
imperialyarn.com;
imperialstockranch.com

The Imperial Stock Ranch is a family-owned and operated ranch located in Oregon's high desert. Established in 1871 and owned by Dan and Jeanne Carver, the ranch has been raising sheep throughout its history; its crossbreeding efforts in the 1880s were instrumental in the development of the Columbia breed.

Imperial Stock Ranch began as a 160-acre homestead claim and grew into one of Oregon's largest ranching empires, and one of the largest sheep operations in the American West. The ranch headquarters are a National Historic District.

For many decades, the ranch's philosophy has been mindful land stewardship— it is simply a way of life that has spanned generations.

The ranch works under a total conservation management plan, which includes environmentally friendly farming and livestock practices, and is a Certified Conservation Farm, having received numerous awards for excellence in land management practices. The sheep graze freely on natural range lands as nature intended, converting the "sunlight energy" from plants into wool, a renewable fiber. The wool is then custom milled into yarns without using harsh chemicals or extreme temperatures, leaving it comfortable, soft and pure.

For most of the ranch's history, wool was sold as a commodity. In the late 1990s, a number of factors contributed to new directions for Imperial Stock Ranch wool. Only in recent years has the Imperial Stock Ranch offered its "sunlight fiber" in the form of natural wool yarns. Their yarns are part of their ranching culture in which history, authenticity and sustainability are a way of life.

1. Columbia sheep
2. Proprietors Dan and Jeanne Carver
3. Welcome!
4. Working dogs

IMPERIAL STOCK RANCH

EST 1871

Straits of Mackinac Vest

◀■■▭

SIZES
Instructions are written for Small. Changes for Medium, Large and X-Large are in parentheses.

FINISHED MEASUREMENTS
BUST (closed) 34 (37, 40, 43)"/86.5 (94, 101.5, 109)cm
LENGTH 25 (25½, 26½, 27½)"/63.5 (65, 67.5, 70)cm

MATERIALS
■ 3 (4, 4, 4) 4oz/113g hanks (each approx 240yd/219m) of Imperial Stock Ranch *Pencil Roving* (wool) in canyon shadow blue (5)
■ 2yd/2m of DK or worsted-weight yarn in matching color (for sewing)
■ Size 13 (9mm) circular needles, 16"/41cm and 36"/91cm long *or size to obtain gauge*
■ One pair size 13 (9mm) needles
■ Cable needle (cn)
■ Stitch holders
■ Stitch markers
■ Three 1¼"/31mm buttons

GAUGE
10 sts and 14 rows to 4"/10cm over reverse St st using size 13 (9mm) circular needle.
12 sts and 15 rows to 4"/10cm over cable pat using size 13 (9mm) needles. *Take time to check gauge.*

This vest is the result of combining two of Amy Polcyn's favorite things about knitting: cables and avoiding seams. She chose simple cables that wouldn't be overwhelmed by the bulkiness of the yarn and kept the knitting interesting by using them in unexpected ways. The result is cozy, cute and quick to knit! This vest would be perfect to wear on a crisp fall day for a walk along the shores of the Great Lakes.

NOTES
1) The waistband is worked first.
2) The lower body is worked from the waistband down and the upper body is worked from the waistband up.

STITCH GLOSSARY
6-st LC Sl next 3 sts to cn and hold to **front**, k3, k3 from cn.

CABLE PATTERN
(worked over 10 sts)
Rows 1 and 3 (RS) P2, k6, p2.
Rows 2 and 4 K2, p6, k2.
Row 5 P2, 6-st LC, p2.
Row 6 K2, p6, k2.
Rep rows 1–6 for cable pat.

VEST
WAISTBAND
With straight needles, cast on 10 sts. Work in cable pat until piece measures 32 (35, 38, 41)"/81 (89, 96.5, 104)cm from beg, end with a WS row. Bind off.

LOWER BODY
With longer circular needle, pick up and k 84 (92, 100, 108) sts evenly spaced along one long edge of waistband.
Next row (WS) K 21 (23, 25, 27) sts, pm, k 42 (46, 50, 54) sts, pm, k 21 (23, 25, 27) sts. Cont in reverse St st and work even for 5"/12.5cm, end with a WS row.
Next (inc) row (RS) *Purl to 1 st before st marker, M1 p-st, p1, sl marker, p1, M1 p-st; rep from * once more, purl to end—88 (96, 104, 112) sts. Work even for 9 rows.
Rep inc row. Work even on 92 (100, 108, 116) sts until piece measures 10 (10,10½,11)"/25.5 (25.5, 26.5, 28)cm from waistband, end with a WS row. Cont in garter st (knit every row) for 1"/2.5cm, end with a WS row. Bind off all sts loosely purlwise.

UPPER BODY
With longer circular needle, pick up and k 84 (92, 100, 108) sts evenly spaced along opposite long edge of waistband. Knit next row. Cont in reverse St st and work even for 3"/7.5cm, end with a WS row.

FOR SMALL SIZE ONLY
BEG FRONT NECK SHAPING
Bind off 6 sts at beg of next 2 rows—72 sts.

DIVIDE FOR FRONTS AND BACK

Cont to shape neck as foll:

Next row (RS) P2tog, purl until there are 12 sts on RH needle, place these 12 sts on holder for right front, bind off next 6 sts (right underarm), purl until there are 36 sts on RH needle (back), bind off next 6 sts (left underarm), purl to last 2 sts, p2tog, place these last 12 sts on holder for left front. *Do not cut yarn.*

BACK

Change to straight needles. Rejoin yarn. Knit next row.

ARMHOLE SHAPING

Dec 1 st each side on next row, then every other row twice more—30 sts. Work even until armhole measures 4"/10cm, end with a WS row.

BACK NECK SHAPING

Next row (RS) P9, join a 2nd ball of yarn and bind off center 12 sts, purl to end. Working both sides at once, knit next row. Dec 1 st from each neck edge on next row, then every other row 6 times more. Work even on 2 sts each side until armhole measures 8"/20.5cm. Bind off each side for shoulders.

LEFT FRONT

Place 12 sts from left front holder on straight needles ready for a WS row. Knit next row.

NECK AND ARMHOLE SHAPING

Cont to dec 1 st from neck edge on next row, then every other row 6 times more. AT THE SAME TIME, dec 1 st from armhole edge on next row, then every other row twice more. Work even on 2 sts until piece measures same length as back to shoulder. Bind off.

RIGHT FRONT

Place 12 sts from right front holder on straight needles ready for a WS row. Rejoin yarn. Knit next row. Cont to work same as left front, reversing shaping.

FOR MEDIUM SIZE ONLY
DIVIDE FOR FRONTS AND BACK, AND BEG FRONT NECK SHAPING

Next row (RS) Bind off 6 sts, purl until there are 14 sts on RH needle, place these 14 sts on holder for right front, bind off next 6 sts (right underarm), purl until there are 40 sts on RH needle (back), bind off next 6 sts (left underarm), purl to end, place last 20 sts on holder for left front. Do not cut yarn.

BACK

Change to straight needles. Rejoin yarn. Knit next row.

ARMHOLE SHAPING

Dec 1 st each side on next row, then every other row 3 times more—32 sts. Work even until armhole measures 4½"/11.5cm, end with a WS row.

BACK NECK SHAPING

Next row (RS) P10, join a 2nd ball of yarn and bind off center 12 sts, purl to end. Working both sides at once, knit next row. Dec 1 st from each neck edge on next row, then every other row 6 times more. Work even on 3 sts each side until armhole measures 8½"/21.5cm. Bind off each side for shoulders.

LEFT FRONT

Place 20 sts from left front holder on straight needles ready for a WS row.

NECK AND ARMHOLE SHAPING

Next row (WS) Bind off first 6 sts, knit to end—14 sts. Dec 1 st from neck edge on next row, then every other row 6 times more. AT THE SAME TIME, dec 1 st from armhole edge on next row, then every other row three times more. Work even on 3 sts until piece measures same length as back to shoulder. Bind off.

RIGHT FRONT

Place 14 sts from right front holder on straight needles ready for a WS row. Rejoin yarn. Knit next row.

NECK AND ARMHOLE SHAPING

Dec 1 st from neck edge on next row, then every other row 6 times more. AT THE SAME TIME, dec 1 st from armhole edge on next row, then every other row three times more. Work even on 3 sts until piece measures same length as back to shoulder. Bind off.

FOR LARGE AND X-LARGE SIZES ONLY
DIVIDE FOR FRONTS AND BACK

Next row (RS) P 22 (23), place these 22 (23) sts on holder for right front, bind off next 6 (8) sts (right underarms), purl until there are 44 (46) sts on RH needle (back), bind off next 6 (8) sts (left underarm), purl to end, place last 22 (23) sts on holder for left front. *Do not cut yarn.*

BACK
Change to straight needles. Rejoin yarn. Knit next row.

ARMHOLE SHAPING
Dec 1 st each side on next row, then every other row 3 times more—36 (38) sts. Work even until armhole measures 5 (5½)"/12.5 (14)cm, end with a WS row.

BACK NECK SHAPING
Next row (RS) P 12 (13), join a 2nd ball of yarn and bind off center 12 sts, purl to end. Working both sides at once, knit next row. Dec 1 st from each neck edge on next row, then every other row 6 times more. Work even on 5 (6) sts each side until armhole measures 9 (9½)"/23 (24)cm. Bind off each side for shoulders.

LEFT FRONT
Place 22 (23) sts from left front holder on straight needles ready for a WS row. Knit next row.

ARMHOLE AND NECK SHAPING
Dec 1 st from armhole edge on next row, then every other row 3 times more. AT THE SAME TIME, when armhole measures ½ (1)"/1.5 (2.5)cm, end with a RS row.
Next row (WS) Bind off first 6 sts, knit to end. Dec 1 st from neck edge on next row, then every other row 6 times more. Work even on 5 (6) sts until piece measures same length as back to shoulder. Bind off.

RIGHT FRONT
Place 22 (23) sts from right front holder on straight needles ready for a WS row. Rejoin yarn. Knit next row.

ARMHOLE AND NECK SHAPING
Cont to work same as left front, reversing all shaping.

FINISHING
Lightly block piece to measurements. Sew shoulders seams using DK or worsted-weight yarn.

NECKBAND
With straight needles, cast on 8 sts. Cont in cable pat as foll:
Rows 1 and 3 (RS) P2, k6.
Rows 2 and 4 P6, k2.
Row 5 P2, 6-st LC.
Row 6 P6, k2. Rep rows 1–6 until piece measures 38"/96.5cm from beg, end with a WS row. Bind off. Sew straight edge of neckband to neck edge using DK or worsted-weight yarn. Place markers for 3 buttonholes along right front edge, with the first in center of waistband, the last in center of neckband and the other evenly spaced between.

BUTTONHOLE BAND
With RS facing and straight needles, pick up and k 41 (43, 46, 49) sts evenly spaced along right front edge. Knit next row.
Next (buttonhole) row (RS) *Knit to marker, bind off next 2 sts; rep from * twice more, knit to end.
Next row Knit, casting on 2 sts over bound-off sts. Cont in garter st for

2 rows more. Bind off all sts loosely knitwise.

BUTTONBAND
With RS facing and straight needles, pick up and k 41 (43, 46, 49) sts evenly spaced along left front edge. Work in garter st for 5 rows. Bind off all sts loosely knitwise.

ARMHOLE EDGING
With RS facing and shorter circular needle, skip first 3 (3, 3, 4) sts of underarm bind-off, pick up and k 40 (43, 45, 49) sts evenly spaced around entire armhole edge. Join and pm for beg of rnd. Purl next rnd. Bind off all sts loosely knitwise. Sew on buttons. ●

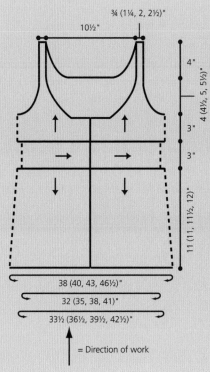

¾ (1¼, 2, 2½)"
10½"
4"
4 (4½, 5, 5½)"
3"
3"
11 (11, 11½, 12)"
38 (40, 43, 46½)"
32 (35, 38, 41)"
33½ (36½, 39½, 42½)"
= Direction of work

Beautiful yarns one skein at a time

Company Stats

COMPANY STARTED
2008

PROPRIETOR
Catherine Petitti

LOCATION
Pasadena, California

YARNS
Eight types, all made in the United States

BUSINESS PHILOSOPHY
To create high-quality handpainted yarn, provide service and support to the retail stores, and develop designs and patterns that give the customer a knitting experience that is unique and satisfying.

WEBSITE
redbarnyarn.com

With a background that includes business ownership, management, and retail and professional services, Catherine Petitti understands precisely what yarn shops deal with and has designed her company with their success as a primary benchmark.

She goes the extra distance to create a product and patterns that make for repeat sales for the retailers in mind. She wants the knitters to enjoy projects that are fun, satisfying and successful and regularly checks in with shop owners for feedback, to support them and to offer ideas from her own retail experience.

Red Barn Yarn was born from a love of fabrics, fibers, textiles and color. Working with natural fibers and high-quality goods only, Petitti mixes all the formulas and does all the painting and coloring herself skein by skein. Colors available are inspired by nature and places on the planet. New colors pop up routinely, and custom colors are also offered. Her palette is marked by tonal sophistication, one of her favorites being her colorway "Pansy." Every little knit stitch turns into a slightly different color of purple, creating a treat for the eye up close and a lovely, rich finished product when seen from a distance. Being an oil painter, Petitti likens her colorways to paintings on wool. Used individually or in combination with the tonal solids, they are an expression of the passion she feels for color.

Petitti is currently searching for American mills and farms with whom to develop her entire line of yarn bases.

1. Owner Catherine Petitti
2. Yarn drying in the California sun
3. The dyeing room
4. Color inspiration

■ RED BARN YARN

Gloucester Wrap

■◀■■▭

SIZES
Instructions are written for size X-Small/Small. Changes for size Medium/Large are in parentheses.

FINISHED MEASUREMENTS
BUST (closed) 36 (40)"/91.5 (101.5)cm
LENGTH 24 (26¾)"/61 (68)cm
UPPER ARM 13 (15)"/33 (38)cm

MATERIALS
■ 10 (14) 4oz/113g hanks (each approx 125yd/114m) of Red Barn Yarn *Bulky* (wool/mohair) in lobelia 🔵
■ Size 11 (8mm) circular needle, 32"/81cm long *or size to obtain gauge*
■ One pair size 11 (8mm) needles *or size to obtain gauge*
■ Cable needle (cn)
■ Stitch markers

GAUGE
15 sts and 17 rows = 4"/10cm over cable pat using size 11 (8mm) circular needle.
12 sts and 16 rows = 4"/10cm over St st using size 11 (8mm) needles. *Take time to check gauge.*

NOTE
Body of sweater is made in one piece from left front edge to right front edge.

When designing this garment, Kirsten Kapur was inspired by coastal New England. Named for the Massachusetts fishing town, the Gloucester Wrap is the perfect garment to throw over jeans and a T-shirt for an evening clambake at the beach. The sweater's cable pattern evokes traditional fisherman's sweaters, but its construction is modern. It can be worn with one end wrapped around the neck, open with both sides hanging down like a cardigan or with a shawl pin fastening the front edges.

STITCH GLOSSARY
8-st LC Sl 4 sts to cn and hold in *front*, k4, k4 from cn.

SEED STITCH
(over an even number of sts)
Row 1 (RS) Slip 1 wyib, k1, *p1, k1, rep from * to end.
Row 2 Slip 1 wyib, p1, *k1, p1; rep from * to end.
Rep rows 1 and 2 for seed st.

CABLE PATTERN
(multiple of 10 sts plus 2)
Row 1 (RS) K2, *8-st LC, k2; rep from * to end.
Rows 2, 4, 6 and 8 Purl.
Rows 3, 5, 7 and 9 Knit.
Row 10 Purl.
Rep rows 1–10 for cable pat.

BODY
LEFT FRONT
Beg at left front edge, with circular needle, cast on 86 (96) sts. *Do not join.* Working back and forth, rep rows 1 and 2 of seed st 6 times.
Next row (RS) Work in seed st over first 7 sts, pm, knit to last 7 sts, pm, work in seed st over last 7 sts.
Next row Work in seed st over first 7 sts, sl marker, purl to next marker, sl marker, work in seed st over last 7 sts. Slipping marker every row, rep last 2 rows twice more. Cont in cable pat as foll:
Row 1 (RS) Work in seed st over first 7 sts, sl marker, work row 1 of cable pat to next marker, sl marker, work in seed st over last 7 sts. Keeping 7 sts each side in seed st as established, work center 72 (82) sts in cable pat to row 10, then rep rows 1–10 of cable pat 8 (9) times more, then rows 1–4 once.

LEFT ARMHOLE SHAPING
Next row (RS) Work in seed st over first 7 sts, sl marker, work row 5 of cable pat over next 39 (45) sts, join a 2nd ball of yarn and bind off next 24 (28) sts, work row 5 over next 9 sts, sl marker, work in seed st over last 7 sts.
Next 3 rows Working both sides at once, work 7 sts each side in seed st and work rows 6–8 of cable pat over rem sts.

Next row (RS) Work in seed st over first 7 sts, sl marker, work row 9 of cable pat over next 39 (45) sts, with same ball of yarn, cast on 24 (28) sts, work row 9 over next 9 sts, sl marker, work in seed st over last 7 sts. Cut 2nd ball of yarn.
Next row (WS) Work in seed st over first 7 sts, sl marker, work row 10 of cable pat over next 72 (82) sts, sl marker, work in seed st over last 7 sts.

BACK

Keeping 7 sts each side in seed st as established, work center 72 (82) sts in cable pat, rep rows 1–10 of cable pat 5 (6) times, then rows 1–4 once.

RIGHT ARMHOLE SHAPING

Work as for left armhole shaping.

RIGHT FRONT

Keeping 7 sts each side in seed st as established, work center 72 (82) sts in cable pat, rep rows 1–10 of cable pat 9 (10) times, then rows 1–4 once.
Next row (RS) Work in seed st over first 7 sts, knit to last 7 sts, work in seed st over last 7 sts.
Next row Work in seed st over first 7 sts, purl to next marker, work in seed st over last 7 sts. Rep last 2 rows twice more.
Next row (RS) Work row 1 of seed st across all sts, dropping markers. Work row 2 of seed st, then rep rows 1 and 2 five times more. Bind off knitwise.

SLEEVES

With straight needles cast on 28 (30) sts.
Row 1 (RS) *K1, p1; rep from * to end.
Row 2 K the purl sts and p the knit sts. Rep row 2 for seed st and work even for 2½"/6.5cm, end with a WS row. Cont in St st and work even for 4 rows.
Inc row (RS) K1, M1, knit to last st, M1, k1. Rep inc row every 8th row 0 (8) times more, every 10th row 2 (0) times, then every 12th row 3 (0) times—38 (46) sts. Work even until piece measures 18"/45.5cm from beg, end with a WS row.

CAP SHAPING

Bind off 3 sts at beg of next 2 rows.
Dec row (RS) K1, ssk, knit to last 3 sts, k2tog, k1. Work next row even. Rep last 2 rows 3 times more—24 (32) sts. Work even for 6 rows. Rep dec row—22 (30) sts. Work even for 3 (1) rows. Rep dec row on next row, then every other row 5 (8) times more, end with a WS row—10 (12) sts. Rep dec row once more. Bind off rem 8 (10) sts purlwise.

FINISHING

Block pieces to measurements. Sew sleeve seams. Set in sleeves. ●

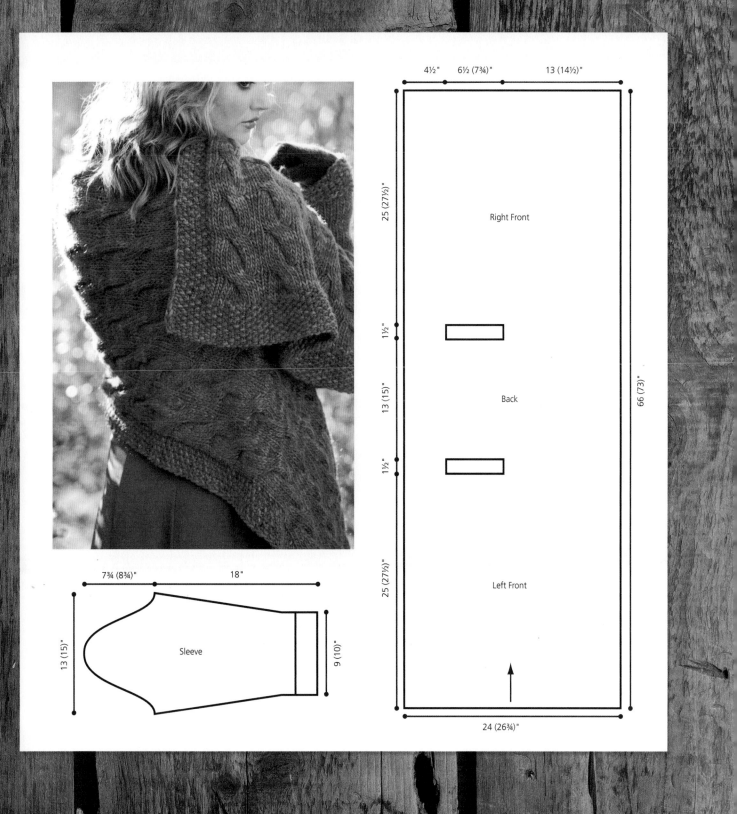

4½" 6½ (7¾)" 13 (14½)"

25 (27½)"

Right Front

1½"

13 (15)"

Back

1½"

66 (73)"

25 (27½)"

Left Front

24 (26¾)"

7¾ (8¾)" 18"

13 (15)"

Sleeve

9 (10)"

Two heads are better than one

Company Stats

COMPANY STARTED
2004

PROPRIETORS
Mary Arnold and Colleen East

LOCATION
Cave Creek, Arizona

YARNS
Eleven types, one made in the USA

BUSINESS PHILOSOPHY

To supply luxurious and affordable handpainted yarns for the knitting, crocheting and weaving communities, while valuing the intimate settings of local yarn stores and continuing to support them.

WEBSITE
conjoinedcreations.com

Conjoined Creations offers colors from bright to subdued, calling them "colors with attitude." Mary Arnold and Colleen East find the interaction and comments from the consumers helpful and custom orders are encouraged: They can match colors from a paint chip, piece of ribbon, or other yarns. All their colorways are named with the 1960s in mind.

Growing up on opposite sides of the country, these two women found each other at a local guild meeting after both moved to Arizona. Discovering that they had similar interests in starting a business, Mary and Colleen put their heads together, bringing skills such as weaving, quilting, dyeing and spinning to the table. Their powerful combination of talents prompted people to ask if they "were joined at the hip." They started to experiment with remnant pieces and various textile mediums

and soon created SOYSILK Fusion Kits. SOYSILK is considered a "green" product, manufactured from the byproduct of tofu with completely exhausted dyes which have no remaining chemicals. These kits are second-generation recycled and kid-safe.

In 2008 they introduced their "Flat Feet" concept, based on a manufacturing design from the 1930s. The yarn does not come in skeins or balls but is instead machine-knit into a sheet that knitters unravel and knit from as they go. Mary's husband works in construction and was given the task of "test-wearing" heels knit up from this fiber; he literally wore them to shreds to determine pilling, lack of shaping, washability, color retention, ease of dyeing, accessibility and affordability. After sending twenty-four flats to knitters across the country for test-knitting and critiquing, adjustments were made and Conjoined Creations' new line was born.

With a variety of yarn weights from lace to bulky in a range of fibers and blends, their yarns are soft, sumptuous and delightful to the touch, complementing well-crafted patterns from nationally known designers to support all yarns.

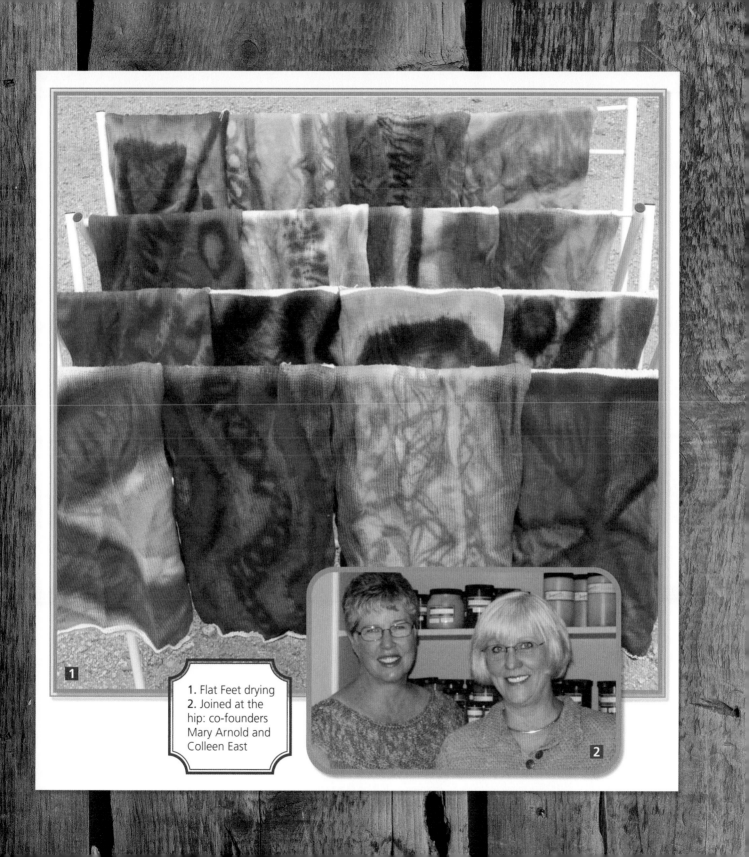

1. Flat Feet drying
2. Joined at the hip: co-founders Mary Arnold and Colleen East

CONJOINED CREATIONS

Evergreen Ankle Socks

◼◼◼◻

SIZES
Instructions are written for Woman's size Medium. Changes for size Large are in parentheses.

FINISHED MEASUREMENTS
FOOT CIRCUMFERENCE
7½"/19cm
FOOT LENGTH
8 (9)"/20.5 (23)cm
SOCK HEIGHT
7¼"/18.5cm

MATERIALS
◼ 1 7oz/200g sheet (each approx 800yd/732m) of Conjoined Creations *Flat Feet Foursome* (superwash merino wool/nylon) in kayla (1)
◼ One set (5) size 1 (2.25mm) double-pointed needles (dpns) *or size to obtain gauge*
◼ Stitch marker

GAUGE
34 sts and 50 rnds to 4"/10cm over St st using size 1 (2.25mm) dpns. *Take time to check gauge.*

NOTE
To work in the rnd, always read chart from right to left.

Faith Hale's parents live on gorgeous farmland in New Jersey not far from where she grew up. Upon receiving this yarn, she was immediately reminded of the Christmas trees her parents sell every year. What better way to represent the Garden State than with lace that looks like tiny trees!

SOCK (make 2)
CUFF
Cast on 64 sts. Divide sts over 4 needles (16 sts on each). Join, taking care not to twist sts on needles, pm for beg of rnds. Work in k1, p1 rib for 1¼"/3cm.

BEG CHART PAT
Rnd 1 Work 16-st rep 4 times. Cont to foll chart in this way to rnd 20, then rep rnds 1–20 once more.

BEG HEEL FLAP
NOTE Heel flap is worked back and forth on one needle over half the sts; rem sts are on hold.
Next row (RS) Sl 1, k31; turn.
Next row Sl 1, p31; turn. Rep these 2 rows 14 time more—15 sl sts along each side edge of heel flap. Turn heel.
Row 1 (RS) K17, ssk, k1; turn.
Row 2 Sl 1, p3, p2tog, p1; turn.
Row 3 Sl 1, k4, ssk, k1; turn.
Row 4 Sl 1, p5, p2tog, p1; turn.
Row 5 Sl 1, k6, ssk, k1; turn.

Row 6 Sl 1, p7, p2tog, p1; turn.
Row 7 Sl 1, k8, ssk, k1; turn.
Row 8 Sl 1, p9, p2tog, p1; turn.
Row 9 Sl 1, k10, ssk, k1; turn.
Row 10 Sl 1, p11, p2tog, p1; turn.
Row 11 Sl 1, k12, ssk, k1; turn.
Row 12 Sl 1, p13, p2tog, p1; turn.
Row 13 Sl 1, k14, ssk, k1; turn.
Row 14 Sl 1, p15, p2tog, p1; turn—18 heel sts.

GUSSET
Working yarn is located at center of heel. When working rnd 1 of gusset, needles will be designated as: *Needle* 1, *Needle* 2, *Needle* 3 and *Needle* 4.
Rnd 1 With *Needle* 1, knit rem 9 sts of heel flap, then pick up and k 15 sts along side edge of heel flap (1 st in each sl st) and 1 st between top of heel flap and held instep sts; with *Needles* 2 and 3, k 32 sts of instep (rnd 1 of chart pat); with *Needle* 4, pick up and k 1 st between instep sts and top of heel flap, then k 15 sts along side edge of heel flap, knit rem 9 sts of heel flap—82 sts (25 sts each on *Needles* 1 and 4, and 16 sts each on *Needles* 2 and 3).
Rnd 2 *Needle* 1 k9, k14 tbl, k2tog; *Needles* 2 and 3 work rnd 2 of chart pat; *Needle* 4 ssk, k14 tbl, k9—80 sts.
Rnd 3 *Needle* 1 knit to end; *Needles* 2 and 3 work next rnd of chart pat; *Needle* 4 k to end.
Rnd 4 *Needle* 1 knit to last 2 sts, k2tog; *Needles* 2 and 3 work next

rnd of chart pat; Needle 4 ssk, knit to end.

Rep rnds 3 and 4 seven times more—64 sts (16 sts on each needle).

FOOT

Cont in pats as established (*Needles* 1 and 4 in St st and *Needles* 2 and 3 in chart pat) until foot of sock measures 6½ (7½)"/16.5 (19)cm or 1½"/4cm shorter than desired length from heel to toe, end with chart pat rnd 1, 10 or 11. (Try on sock to ensure the correct length.)

TOE

Next rnd Knit.

Dec rnd *Needle* 1 knit to last 3 sts, k2tog, k1; *Needle* 2 k1, ssk, knit to end; *Needle* 3 knit to last 3 sts, k2tog, k1; *Needle* 4 k1, ssk, knit to end.

Rep these 2 rnds 8 times more—28 sts.

Next rnd With *Needle* 4, knit to end of *Needle* 1; sl sts from *Needle* 2 to *Needle* 3.

Graft sts on *Needle* 3 to sts on *Needle* 4 using Kitchener stitch (see page 139, opposite). ●

KITCHENER STITCH

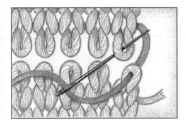

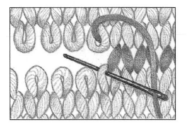

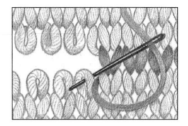

1 Insert the yarn needle purlwise into the first stitch on the front piece, then knitwise into the first stitch on the back piece. Draw the yarn through.

2 Insert the yarn needle knitwise into the first stitch on the front piece again. Draw the yarn through.

3 Insert the needle purlwise into the next stitch on the front piece. Draw the yarn through.

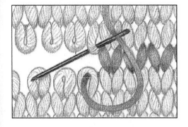

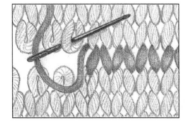

4 Insert the yarn needle purlwise into the first stitch on the back piece again. Draw the yarn through.

5 Inert the yarn needle knitwise into the next stitch on the back piece. Draw the yarn through. Repeat steps 2 through 5.

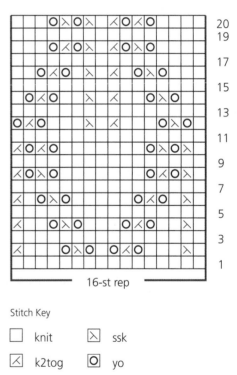

16-st rep

20
19
17
15
13
11
9
7
5
3
1

Stitch Key

☐ knit ☒ ssk

☒ k2tog ⊙ yo

A jewel of a yarn

Company Stats

COMPANY STARTED
2005; incorporated in 2006

PROPRIETOR
Carl and Eileen Koop

LOCATION
Elbert, Colorado

YARNS
Pure yak as well as blends of yak, Cormo wool, alpaca and bamboo in yarn and roving

BUSINESS PHILOSOPHY
To produce and raise awareness about premium yak fiber products, with hopes to expand the ranching community in the U.S. and help support the nomadic herds of Tibet, Nepal and Mongolia.

WEBSITE
bijoubasinranch.com

Bijou Basin Ranch is a working yak ranch on the open plains of Colorado and is the only company in the United States that exclusively promotes high-quality yak fiber and yarn.

Owners Carl and Eileen Koop previously worked in highly technical fields but sought to embrace a simpler lifestyle. They found yaks to be great pasture animals—easy to care for, hardy and not too big—that provide multiple opportunities for business endeavors. Carl and Eileen quickly settled on exploring the fiber market for yaks, as it was virtually unknown. (Yak were first imported to North America in the late 1920s; however, close to 100 years later, there are still only a few thousand animals in America today.)

The Koops' primary goal became to produce and sell premium yak fiber products such as roving, yarn and yarn blends. They supplement their stock by buying quality yak fiber from other ranchers across the county and abroad. The fiber is then processed into yarn at various mills across the country or abroad.

Typically, yak produce two different types of hair. The first is the outer "guard hair" which is the longer, coarser, stronger hair. The longest and strongest guard hair is found on the animal's tail and "skirt." Because of their strength and coarse nature, the guard hairs are typically carded and then worsted-spun. They are then braided into ropes, halters and belts or woven into very durable rugs and bags.

The second type of hair is the short, fine, soft undercoat or "down hair," which is produced by the animals during the winter and is an incredible insulator. The down is shed in the spring and is harvested by combing.

The down is an extremely durable and lightweight fiber that preserves heat in the winter yet breathes for comfort in warmer weather. Yak yarn is completely odorless, does not shed and maintains warmth even when wet. The yarn is non-allergenic and non-irritating, as it contains no animal oils or residue.

To satisfy the needs of spinners, knitters and weavers, Bijou Basin Ranch carries a variety of fiber products, using numerous small mills throughout the United States to produce yarn. While some of the yarn is 100-percent pure yak, other yarn is blended with fibers such as Cormo wool, alpaca and bamboo, coming in various weights and lengths which depend on the particular fiber or fiber blend used.

1. Home on the range
2. Keeping a watchful eye
3. Yakking it up

■ BIJOU BASIN RANCH

Lacy Leaves Scarf

■■■▭

FINISHED MEASUREMENTS
Approx 4¾" x 66"/12cm
x 167.5cm

MATERIALS
■ 2 2oz/56g hanks (each
approx 200yd/183m) of Bijou
Basin Ranch *Himalayan Trail*
(yak/merino wool) in brown ③
■ Size 5 (3.75mm) circular
needles, 40"/101.5cm long *or
size to obtain gauge*

GAUGE
24 sts and 32 rows to 4"/10cm
over St st using size 5 (3.75mm)
circular needle.
Take time to check gauge.

NOTE
Scarf is knit horizontally from
one long side edge to opposite
long side edge.

One of the first things Melissa
LaBarre ever knit without a
pattern was a leaf. She loves
how a few simple increases
and decreases can make a
perfect leafy shape, and even
after years of knitting leaves,
she hasn't grown tired of
incorporating them into her
designs. A leaf motif paired
with a warm, natural fiber is
a match made in heaven.

SCARF
Cast on 391 sts.

BEG CHART PAT
Row 1 (RS) Work 17-st rep 23
times. Cont to foll chart in
this way to row 43. Bind off all
sts loosely knitwise.

FINISHING
Wet-block piece to
measurements, pinning out
points at top of each leaf
column. ●

Stitch Key

☐ k on RS, p on WS

⊟ p on RS, k on WS

◿ k2tog

◺ ssk

⅄ SK2P

○ yo

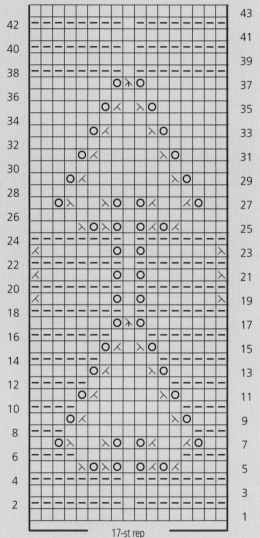

17-st rep

Happy sheep = happy yarns

Company Stats

COMPANY STARTED
2007

PROPRIETOR
Valerie Spanos and
Karen Hostetler

LOCATION
Buffalo, Wyoming

YARNS
Eight types as well as roving,
all made in the United States

BUSINESS PHILOSOPHY

*To create beautiful
wool yarns using
all-natural methods
in order to provide
their customers with
fiber that is baby
soft—and baby safe.*

WEBSITE
mountainmeadowwool.com

When Wyoming's governor was asked what his favorite thing in 2009 was, he declared it to be "my visit to Mountain Meadow Wool." Wyoming is the country's second biggest wool producer, but has very little manufacturing and no textile industry to speak of. Valerie Spanos and Karen Hostetler started Mountain Meadow Wool in an effort to change that.

After receiving funding from the USDA's Small Business Innovative Research Program in 2002, they developed their yarn prototypes using fiber-making equipment from World War II. The only yarn company in the country using only environmentally friendly processing in 100-percent domestic, 100-percent traceable and 100-percent natural wool products, they believe they can create beautiful and natural wools using all-natural methods. Because the sheep ranchers (many of whom are friends and neighbors) maintain ownership of the fiber until it is sold as yarn, they feel a connection to the knitter and encourage positive handling of the ranches and animals. Mountain Meadow's motto is "beautiful yarns come from happy sheep and happy sheep are treated with kindness and care." By supporting their local ranchers and using only wool from open-range sheep, they feel they are helping to preserve open spaces in the West.

The dry climate, clean air, cool summers and cold winters of Wyoming make the wool naturally soft. Only accepting wool with a micron count of less than 23, Mountain Meadow keeps Rambouillet as their primary breed with an occasional Columbia or Targhee. The source of each hank of yarn is traceable, for it is labeled with the ranch it came from.

1. Owner Valerie Spanos cuddles a new addition
2. Feeding time
3. Rambouillet ram

WEST

▦ Mountain Meadow Wool

Dreaming of Spring Mittens

▪▪▪▪

SIZE
Instructions are written for one size.

FINISHED MEASUREMENTS
Hand circumference 8"/20.5cm
Length of cuff approx 2"/5cm

MATERIALS
▪ 1 2oz/57g hank (approx
200yd/181m) of Mountain Meadow
Wool *Kettle-Dyed Artisan
Cody* (mountain merino wool) each
in coconut (A), sky (B) and
crimson (C) ⟨2⟩
▪ Contrasting DK-weight yarn
(waste yarn)
▪ One set (5) each size 3 (3.25mm)
double-pointed needles (dpns) *or
size to obtain gauge*
▪ Stitch marker

GAUGE
26 sts and 29 rnds to 4"/10cm
over St st and chart pats using size
3 (3.25mm) dpns.
Take time to check gauge.

NOTE
To work in the rnd, always read
charts from right to left.

Ellie Stubenrauch grew up in
western Michigan and was
inspired by the mitten-shaped
peninsula of her youth in
designing these pretty
handwarmers. The state bird of
Michigan is the American robin,
and she has always had a soft
spot for these abundant and
cheerfully colored songsters. One
of the first heralds of warmer
weather, the robin is a reminder
that spring will be here soon.

STITCH GLOSSARY
kfb Knit in front and back of st—1
st increased.
M1R (make 1 right) Insert left needle
from *back* to *front* into the
horizontal strand between the last
st worked and the next st on left
needle. Using color indicated on
chart, knit this strand through the
front loop to twist the st.
M1L (make 1 left) Insert left needle
from *front* to *back* into the
horizontal strand between the last
st worked and the next st on left
needle. Using color indicated on
chart, knit this strand through the
back loop to twist the st.

CORRUGATED RIB
(multiple of 2 sts)
Rnd 1 *K1 with A, p1 with B; rep
from * around.
Rep rnd 1 for corrugated rib.

LEFT MITTEN
CUFF
With A, cast on 440 sts. Divide sts
over 4 needles (110 sts on each).
Join, taking care not to twist sts on
needles, pm for beg of rnds. Cont
in corrugated rib for 16 rnds. With
A, knit next rnd.
Next (inc) rnd With A, *k4, kfb, k5,
kfb; rep from * around—52 sts.
Cont in St st as foll:

BEG CHART PAT I
Beg chart on rnd 1 and work even
through rnd 2.

THUMB GUSSET
Rnd 3 With A, M1R, k1, M1L, work
to end of rnd—54 sts. Cont to foll
chart in this way through rnd 22,
working inc as shown—72 sts.
Rnd 23 Place 20 thumb sts on scrap
yarn. Cont to work to top of chart,
dec top of mitten as shown—18 sts.
Using A, graft sts tog using
Kitchener st (see page 139).

THUMB
Place 20 sts on scrap yarn evenly
over 4 needles (5 sts on each). Pm
for beg of rnds. Rejoin A, leaving a
long tail for sewing.

BEG CHART II
Beg chart on rnd 1 and work to rnd
8, working inc and dec as shown—
20 sts. Cut B. Cont with A only.
Rnd (dec) 9 [Ssk] 10 times—10 sts.

Chart I

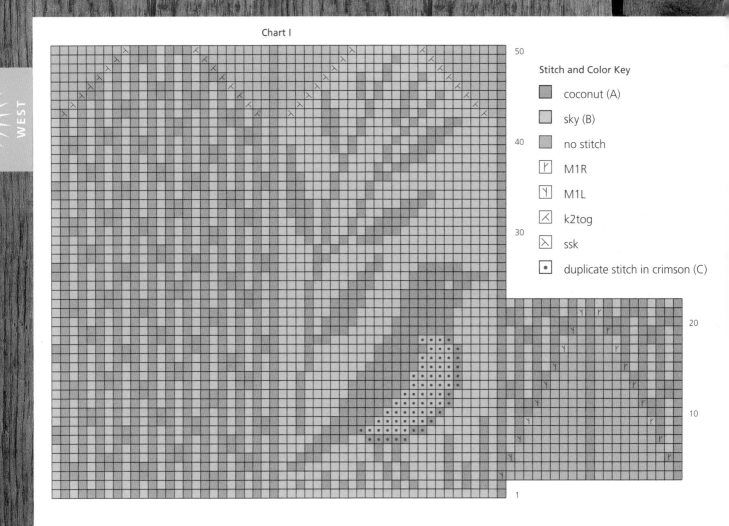

Stitch and Color Key

- ☐ coconut (A)
- ☐ sky (B)
- ☐ no stitch
- M1R
- M1L
- k2tog
- ssk
- ⊡ duplicate stitch in crimson (C)

Chart II

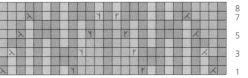

Rnd (dec) 10 [Ssk] 5 times—5 sts. Cut A, leaving a 6"/15.5cm tail. Thread tail in tapestry needle, then thread through rem sts. Pull tog tightly and secure end.

RIGHT MITTEN

CUFF
Work as for left mitten to inc rnd.
Next (inc) rnd With A, *k5,

kfb, k4, kfb; rep from * around—52 sts. Cont to work as for left mitten, foll chart III for hand and chart II for thumb.

FINISHING

Use A tail to sew gap between thumb and hand closed. Add duplicate stitch embroidery. ●

Chart III

DUPLICATE STITCH EMBROIDERY

Using tapestry needle and C, embroider duplicate stitches for robin's red breast, foll chart I for left mitten and chart III for right mitten. Block pieces to measurements.

From recreation to vocation

Company Stats

COMPANY STARTED
2007

PROPRIETORS
Robin and Chuck Page

LOCATION
San Pedro, California

YARNS
Nine types, all made in the United States

BUSINESS PHILOSOPHY
To produce the highest quality handspun and hand-dyed yarns and fibers using traditional handcrafting techniques.

WEBSITE
pagewoodfarm.com

Pagewood Farm grew from Robin and Chuck Page's love of fiber arts. First as hobbyists, they mastered the art of spinning yarns; and after selling their yarns at various venues, they developed a loyal following.

Robin studied under master spinners and dyers to hone her creative abilities and color sense, resulting in completely original colorways and novelty yarns. With a desire to be at the creative lead in the handcrafted fiber industry, the Pages are constantly looking for new yarns and yarn blends and unique colorways so that retail customers can produce beautiful projects using hand-dyed yarn.

Pagewood's fiber comes undyed from small mills following the Pages' exacting yarn specifications, and each yarn blend is tested many times before becoming part of the line. Knowing where their fiber comes from means Robin and Chuck stand behind their line 100 percent.

As their company continued to grow, Robin and Chuck developed a unique dye process to create variegated colorways as well as tone-on-tone solids in small hand-dyed batches that are available in all yarn blends. While still maintaining its handcrafting roots, Pagewood Farm expanded to be featured in yarn shops nationwide, and is now becoming known worldwide, recently adding roving, locks and needle-felting kits to their lineup. New fiber product ideas are a constant crop.

Recently, the Pages discovered unique handspun yarns created by women's collectives in South America. This inspired them to create a new side of the company called the U-Knitted Nations, through which they purchase finished yarns from the collectives and distribute them.

1. The outdoor dyeing area
2. Natural inspiration
3. Jewel tones

■ PAGEWOOD FARM

Betsy Baby Cardigan

■■■◻

SIZES
Instructions are written for size 12 months. Changes for 18 and 24 months are in parentheses.

FINISHED MEASUREMENTS
CHEST (closed) 24 (26, 28)"/61 (66, 71)cm
LENGTH 12 (13½, 14½)"/30.5 (34, 37)cm
UPPER ARM 8 1/2 (9½,10½)"/21.5 (24, 26.5)cmm

MATERIALS
■ 1 (2, 2) 5.5oz/156g hanks (each approx 450yd/411m) of Pagewood Farm *Glacier Bay* (merino superwash) in plum (**2**)
■ Size 5 (3.75mm) circular needle, 24"/61cm long *or size to obtain gauge*
■ One set (5) size 5 (3.75mm) double-pointed needles (dpns)
■ Size E-4 (3.5mm) crochet hook
■ Stitch holders
■ Stitch markers
■ Two ½"/12mm buttons

GAUGE
24 sts and 32 rows to 4"/10cm over St st using size 5 (3.75mm) circular needle.
Take time to check gauge.

NOTE
Body is made in one piece to underarms.

This sweater was inspired by the charming designs for babies that were so popular in the 1950s. Kristen Rengren chose the style because she wanted to make a timeless cardigan that could be passed down from baby to baby.

SEED STITCH (worked in the round) (over an even number of sts)
Rnd 1 *K1, p1; rep from * around.
Rnd 2 K the purl sts and p the knit sts. Rep rnd 2 for seed st.

SEED STITCH (worked back and forth) (over an even number of sts)
Row 1 *K1, p1; rep from * to end.
Row 2 K the purl sts and p the knit sts. Rep row 2 for seed st.

SLEEVES
With dpn, cast on 34 (36, 38) sts dividing sts evenly over 4 needles. Join and pm, taking care not to twist sts on needles. Work around in seed st for 11 rnds. Cont in St st (knit every rnd) as foll:
Inc rnd K1, M1, knit to last st, M1, k1. Rep inc rnd every 4th rnd 4 (6, 8) times more, then every 6th rnd 4 times—52 (58, 64) sts. Work even until piece measures 7½ (8½, 11)"/19 (21.5, 28)cm from beg, end last rnd 6 sts before rnd marker.
Next row K12 (dropping marker), place these sts on scrap yarn for underarm; place rem 40 (46, 52) sts on st holder. Set aside.

BODY
With circular needle, cast on 184 (196, 208) sts. Work back and forth in seed st for 12 rows, end with a WS row.

BEG CHART PAT
Row 1 (RS) Work in seed st over first 8 sts, pm, work 15-st rep twice, pm, k 8 (11, 14), pm, k 92 (98, 104), pm, k 8 (11, 14), pm, work 15-st rep twice, pm, work in seed st over last 8 sts.
Row 2 Work in seed st to first marker, sl marker, work 15-st rep twice, sl marker, p 8 (11, 14), sl marker, p 92 (98, 104), sl marker, p 8 (11, 14), sl marker, work 15-st rep twice, sl marker, work in seed st to end. Keeping 8 sts each side in seed st, 30 sts each front in chart pat and rem sts in St st, cont to foll chart in this way to row 25; when chart is completed, work these sts in St st. AT THE SAME TIME, beg to shape sides on next row as foll:
Dec row (RS) Work in seed st to first marker, sl marker, work 15-st rep twice, sl marker, *knit to 2 sts before next marker, ssk, sl marker, k2tog; rep from * once more, knit to next marker, sl marker, work 15-st rep twice, sl marker, work in seed st to end. Rep dec row every 8th row 2 (2, 3) times more, every 6th row 3 times, every 4th row 2 (3, 2) times, then every other row 2 (1, 1) times—144 (156, 168) sts. Work even until piece measures 7 (8,

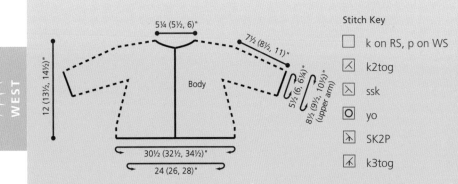

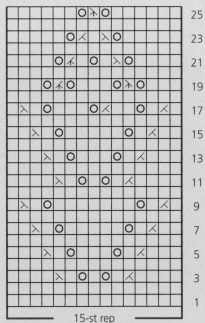

Stitch Key

☐	k on RS, p on WS
◣	k2tog
◢	ssk
○	yo
⋏	SK2P
⋏	k3tog

25
23
21
19
17
15
13
11
9
7
5
3
1

15-st rep

9)"/17.5 (20.5, 23)cm from beg, end with a RS row.

DIVIDE FOR FRONTS AND BACK
Dropping all but first and last markers, work as foll:
Next row (WS) Work in seed st to first marker, sl marker, p 42 (45, 48) sts, place last 12 sts on scrap yarn for underarm, p 72 (78, 84) sts, place last 12 sts on scrap yarn for underarm, purl to last marker, sl marker, work in seed st over last 8 sts—120 (132, 144) sts.

YOKE
Next (joining) row (RS) Work in seed st to first marker, k 21 (24, 27) sts (right front), pm, k1, pm, k 40 (46, 52) sleeve sts, pm, k1, pm, k 58 (64, 70) sts (back), pm, k1, pm, k 40 (46, 52) sleeve sts, pm, k1, pm, k 21 (24, 27) sts (left front), sl marker, work in seed st to end—200 (224, 248) sts.
Next row Work in seed st to first marker, sl marker, purl to last marker, sl marker, work in seed st to end.
Dec row 1 (RS) Work in seed st to first marker, sl marker, *knit to 2 sts before next marker, sl marker, k2tog, sl marker, k1, sl marker, ssk;

rep from * 3 times more, knit to last marker, sl marker, work in seed st to end.
Next row Work in seed st to first marker, sl marker, purl to last marker, sl marker, work in seed st to end. Rep last 2 rows 7 (9, 11) times more—136 (144, 152) sts.
Dropping all but first and last markers, work as foll:
Next row (RS) Work in seed st to end. Rep last row 8 times more, end with a RS row.
Next row (WS) Work in seed st to first marker, sl marker, purl to last marker, sl marker, work in seed st to end.
Dec row 2 (RS) Work in seed st to first marker, sl marker, k 0 (1, 2), *k1, k2tog; rep from *, end k 0 (1, 2), sl marker, work in seed st to end—96 (102, 108) sts.
Next row Work in seed st to first marker, sl marker, purl to last marker, sl marker, work in seed st to end. Work even as established for 2 rows.
Dec row 3 (RS) Work in seed st to first marker, sl marker, k 0 (1, 1), *k2 tog, k1, k2tog; rep from *, end k 0 (0, 1), sl marker, work in seed st to end—64 (68, 72) sts.
Next row Work in seed st to first

marker, sl marker, purl to last marker, sl marker, work in seed st to end.

NECKBAND
Dropping rem markers, work in seed st on all sts for 9 rows. Bind off in seed st.

FINISHING
Block piece to measurements. Graft underarm sts tog using Kitchener st.

BUTTON LOOPS (MAKE 2)
With crochet hook, make a ch 2"/5cm long, join ch with a sl st in first ch. Fasten off, leaving a long tail for sewing. Sew first loop ½"/1.3cm from top right neck edge and ½"/1.3cm in from right front edge. Sew second loop 1"/2.5cm below first loop. Sew on buttons. ●

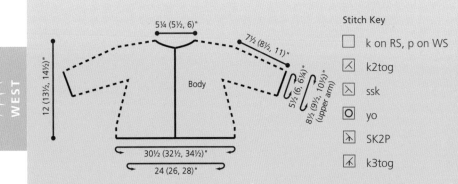

Measurement diagram labels: 5¼ (5½, 6)" · 7½ (8½, 11)" · 12 (13½, 14½)" · Body · 5½ (6, 6¼)" · 8½ (9½, 10½)" (upper arm) · 30½ (32½, 34½)" · 24 (26, 28)"

WEST

■ HAZEL KNITS

Nuts about color

Company Stats

COMPANY STARTED
2007

PROPRIETOR
Wendee Shulsen

LOCATION
Seattle, Washington

YARNS
Three kinds, all dyed in the United States with the base fiber coming from Canada

BUSINESS PHILOSOPHY

To provide the highest-quality yarn in vivid, bold colors to inspire knitters to create their own works of functional art.

WEBSITE
hazelknits.com

From the very first time she picked up a pair of knitting needles and learned to cast on, Wendee Shulsen knew she'd have a future in the yarn industry.

Having always been fascinated by color and loving the feeling of wool moving through her fingers, Shulsen found there was simply no way to stall this new obsession. She took a part-time job at a local yarn store where she noticed that the customers were constantly asking for things the store didn't have, couldn't get or that weren't even being produced. A light bulb went on in her head and Hazel Knits was born.

Hazel Knits yarns are all custom-spun to Shulsen's specifications and she does all of the dyeing herself, using only the highest quality dyes in their purest form so her color palette is clear and bright. An avid rock climber, gardener and outdoor enthusiast, she gets to experience firsthand the majesty of the fauna, water and rocks and translates this beauty to her yarns.

The human eye can identify up to one million colors, and Shulsen is doing her best to make all of these colors attainable in her fibers.

1. Fresh out of the dye pot
2. Yarn drying

HAZEL KNITS

Winterthur Beret and Cowl Set

SIZE
Instructions are written for one size.

FINISHED MEASUREMENTS
BERET
Head circumference 22"/51cm
Depth 8½"/21.5cm
COWL
Neck circumference 20"/51cm
Length 9"/23cm

MATERIALS
■ 1 4oz/113g hank (each approx 275yd/251m) of Hazel Knits *Artisan Lively* (superwash merino wool/nylon) each in lime granita (MC) and olympic rainforest (CC) **3**
■ Size 4 (3.5mm) circular needles, 16"/40cm and 24"/61cm long *or size to obtain gauge*
■ One set (5) size 4 (3.5mm) double-pointed needles (dpns)
■ Stitch marker

GAUGE
24 sts and 26 rnds to 4"/10cm over St st and chart pats using size 4 (3.5mm) circular needle.
Take time to check gauge.

NOTE
To work in the rnd, always read charts from right to left.

With its spectacular gardens and breathtaking art objects, the Winterthur Museum and Estate in Delaware is a wonderful place to visit and inspired Elsbeth Kursh's lovely accessories set. The colors of the yarn reflect the springtime greenery that appears seemingly overnight in the Brandywine River Valley where the historic estate is located.

STITCH GLOSSARY
Dec 3 sts Slip next 2 stitches as if to k2tog, with CC, ssk, then pass the 2 slipped stitches over the stitch remaining from the ssk.

BERET
With shorter circular needle and MC, cast on 99 sts. Join, taking care not to twist sts on needle.
Place marker for end of rnd and sl marker every rnd. Work in k2, p1 rib for 9 rnds.
Next (inc) rnd *K3, M1; rep from * around—132 sts.

BEG CHART PAT I
Rnd 1 Work 4-st rep 33 times. Cont to foll chart in this way to rnd 6, then rep rnds 1–6 seven times more.

CROWN SHAPING
Note Change to dpns (dividing sts evenly between 4 needles) when there are too few sts to work with circular needle.

BEG CHART PAT II
Rnd 1 Work rnd 1 of chart 12 times—96 sts.
Rnds 2 and 3 Work 8-st rep 12 times.
Rnd 4 Work rnd 4 of chart 12 times—60 sts.
Rnds 5 and 6 Work 5-st rep 12 times.
Rnd 7 Work rnd 7 of chart 12 times—24 sts.
Rnd 8 Work 2-st rep 12 times.
Cut MC and cont with CC only.
Next (dec) rnd [Dec 3 sts] 6 times—6 sts. Cut yarn leaving a 8"/20.5cm tail and thread through rem sts.
Pull tog tightly and secure end.

COWL
With longer circular needle and MC, cast on 108 sts. Join, taking care not to twist sts on needle. Place marker for end of rnd and sl marker every rnd. Work in garter st (knit 1 rnd, purl 1 rnd) for 8 rnds.

Next (inc) rnd *K9, M1; rep from *
around—120 sts.

BEG CHART PAT I
Rnd 1 Work 4-st rep 30 times. Cont
to foll chart in this way to rnd 6,
then rep rnds 1–6 nine times more,
then rnds 1–3 once. Cut CC and
cont with MC only.
Next rnd Knit.
Next (dec) rnd *P9, p2tog;
rep from * around—108 sts. Cont
in garter st for 8 rnds. Purl next rnd.
Bind off all sts loosely knitwise.

FINISHING
Block piece lightly to
measurements. ●

Chart I

6
5

3

1

4-st
rep

Chart II

8
7

5

3

1

Stitch and Color Key

☐ no stitch

△3 dec 3 sts

☐ lime granita (MC)

☐ olympic rainforest (CC)

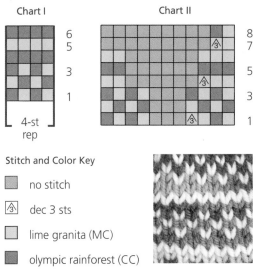

From sheep to knits

Company Stats

COMPANY STARTED
1983

PROPRIETOR
Elsa Hallowell

LOCATION
Bayfield, Colorado

YARNS
Two types, both made In the United States

BUSINESS PHILOSOPHY

The Golden Rule: To treat animals, employees, business associates and customers as we would want to be treated.

WEBSITE
wool-clothing.com

During the 1960s, the biggest part of Elsa Hallowell's livelihood came from working with animals; the other part came from crafting. In the 1970s these two aspects of her life began to converge, and by 1983 they had woven themselves together into a fiber-animal ranch and an animal-fiber business called Elsawool.

Owned and operated by Hallowell, Elsawool's mission is to produce a fiber of the highest caliber that is strong and durable with a high degree of softness. Spending a few years experimenting with various species and breeds of fiber animals, Hallowell learned about Cormo sheep, a breed developed by a geneticist in Australia from superfine merino ewes and Corriedale rams. She knew her search for the right fiber animal was over and she has never looked back.

Today Elsawool sells wool yarns and finished goods. They are made according to Hallowell's specifications and are marketed and sold directly to the consumer, with the wool coming from her purebred Cormo flocks in Colorado and Montana. The yarns retain the natural colors of the fleece. A portion of the yarn is offered to the consumer while the rest of it is made into finished goods.

1. Cormo sheep
2. Gathering the fleece
3. Hallowell with the finished product

■ ELSAWOOL

Oquirrh Mountains Wrap

■■■■

WEST

FINISHED MEASUREMENTS
Approx 74" x 20½"/188cm x 52cm

MATERIALS
■ 3 4oz/113g hanks (each approx 238yd/218m) of Elsawool *Woolen Spun Worsted* (purebred Cormo wool) in white (■4■)
■ One pair size 8 (5mm) needles *or size to obtain gauge*
■ Stitch markers

GAUGE
17 sts and 30 rows to 4"/10cm over garter st using size 8 (5mm) needles (before blocking).
Take time to check gauge.

NOTE
To work in the rnd, always read charts from right to left.

STITCH GLOSSARY
kf&b Inc 1 by knitting into the front and back of the next st.

Every weekday morning, Susan Lawrence commutes from her home in the foothills of the Oquirrh Mountains to downtown Salt Lake City. As she travels west on the freeway in the winter months, the rising sun behind her strikes the mountains in front of her, making the snowy mountaintops appear to glow against the bright blue sky. This stunning wrap was inspired by this beautiful morning view.

WRAP
Loosely cast on 18 sts.
Next row (RS) K3, pm, k13, ssk.
Next row P1, kf&b, k15.

INCREASING SECTION
NOTE On some rows, you will be removing and replacing marker. On all other rows, slip marker as you come to it.
Row 1 (RS) K2tog, yo, k to marker, remove marker, k1, replace marker, k1, yo, k3, yo, k2, p1, k3, yo, k1tbl, k1, ssk.
Row 2 P1, kf&b, k1tbl, yo, k1, p2tog, [yo] twice, [p2tog] twice, yo, p4, k to last 2 sts, p2.
Row 3 K2tog, yo, k to marker, ssk, yo, k5, yo, p2tog, k1, p1, k3, yo, k1tbl, k1, ssk.
Row 4 P1, kf&b, k1tbl, yo, k1, p2tog, [yo] twice, [p2tog] twice, yo, p6, k to last 2 sts, p2.
Row 5 K2tog, yo, k to marker,

remove marker, k1, replace marker, k1, yo, k7, yo, p2tog, k1, p1, k3, yo, k1tbl, k1, ssk.
Row 6 P1, kf&b, k1tbl, yo, k1, p2tog, [yo] twice, [p2tog] twice, yo, p8, k to last 2 sts, p2.
Row 7 K2tog, yo, k to marker, ssk, yo, k6, k2tog, yo, k1, yo, p2tog, k1, p1, k3, yo, k1tbl, k1, ssk.
Row 8 P1, kf&b, k1tbl, yo, k1, p2tog, [yo] twice, [p2tog] twice, yo, k3, yo, p2tog, p5, k to last 2 sts, p2.
Row 9 K2tog, yo, k to marker, remove marker, k1, replace marker, k1, yo, k4, k2tog, yo, k5, yo, p2tog, k1, p1, k3, yo, k1tbl, k1, ssk.
Row 10 P1, kf&b, k1tbl, yo, k1, p2tog, [yo] twice, [p2tog] twice, yo, k7, yo, p2tog, p3, k to last 2 sts, p2.
Row 11 K2tog, yo, k to marker, ssk, yo, k2, k2tog, yo, k9, yo, k3, p1, k3, yo, k1tbl, k1, ssk.
Row 12 P1, k1, k1tbl, yo, k1, p2tog, [yo] twice, p2tog, p3tog, yo, k11, yo, p2tog, p1, k to last 2 sts, p2.
Row 13 K2tog, yo, k to marker, remove marker, k1, replace marker, k1, yo, k3, yo, ssk, k7, k2tog, yo, k4, p1, p2tog, yo, k2, k2tog.
Row 14 P1, k1, p2tog, yo, [p2tog] twice, [yo] twice, p2tog, k1, yo, p2tog, k5, p2tog tbl, yo, p4, k to last 2 sts, p2.
Row 15 K2tog, yo, k to marker, ssk, yo, k5, yo, ssk, k3, k2tog, yo, k1, p2tog, k1, p1, p2tog, yo, k2, k2tog.
Row 16 P1, k1, p2tog, yo, [p2tog] twice, [yo] twice, p2tog, yo, p2tog, k1, p2tog tbl, yo, p6,

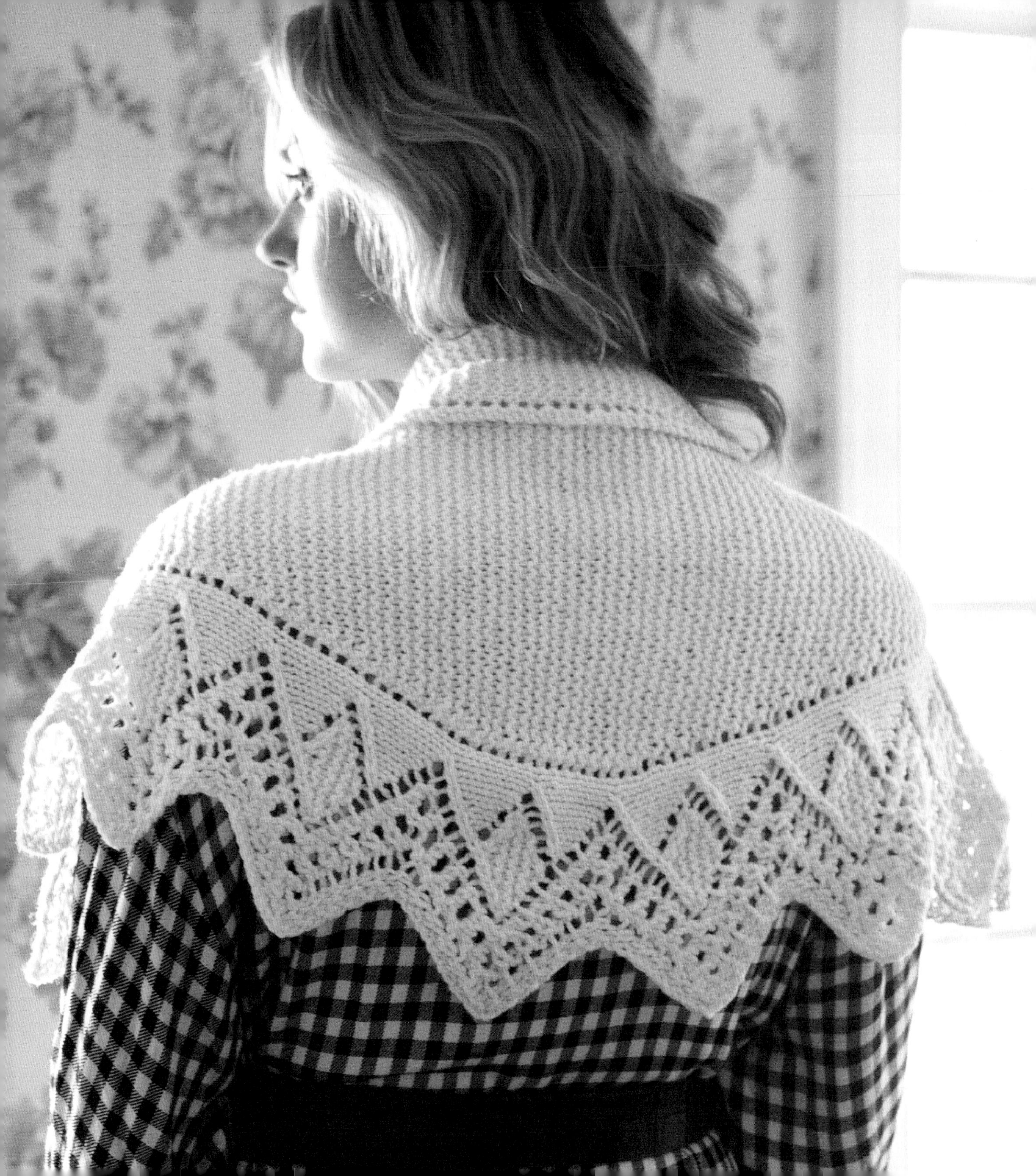

k to last 2 sts, p2.

Row 17 K2tog, yo, k to marker, remove marker, k1, replace marker, k1, yo, k7, yo, k3tog, yo, k3, p1, p2tog, yo, k2, k2tog.

Row 18 P1, k1, p2tog, yo, [p2tog] twice, [yo] twice, p2tog, yo, p2tog, p7, k to last 2 sts, p2.

Row 19 K2tog, yo, k to marker, ssk, yo, k6, k2tog, yo, k3, p1, p2tog, yo, k2, k2tog.

Row 20 P1, k1, p2tog, yo, [p2tog] twice, [yo] twice, p2tog, yo, p2tog, p5, k to last 2 sts, p2.

Row 21 K2tog, yo, k to marker, remove marker, k1, replace marker, k1, yo, k4, k2tog, yo, k3, p1, p2tog, yo, k2, k2tog.

Row 22 P1, k1, p2tog, yo, [p2tog] twice, [yo] twice, p2tog, yo, p2tog, p3, k to last 2 sts, p2.

Row 23 K2tog, yo, k to marker, ssk, yo, k2, k2tog, yo, k3, p1, p2tog, yo, k2, k2tog.

Row 24 P1, kf&b, p2tog, yo, [p2tog] twice, [yo] twice, p2tog, yo, p2tog, p1, k to last 2 sts, p2.

Rep rows 1–24 8 times more.

CENTER SECTION

NOTE Slip marker as you come to it on every row.

Row 1 (RS) K2tog, yo, k to marker, ssk, yo, k3, yo, k2, p1, k3, yo, k1tbl, k1, ssk.

Row 2 P1, kf&b, k1tbl, yo, k1, p2tog, [yo] twice, [p2tog] twice, yo, p4, k to last 2 sts, p2.

Row 3 K2tog, yo, k to marker, ssk, yo, k5, yo, p2tog, k1, p1, k3, yo, k1tbl, k1, ssk.

Row 4 P1, kf&b, k1tbl, yo, k1, p2tog, [yo] twice, [p2tog] twice, yo, p6, k to last 2 sts, p2.

Row 5 K2tog, yo, k to marker, ssk, yo, k7, yo, p2tog, k1, p1, k3, yo, k1tbl, k1, ssk.

Row 6 P1, kf&b, k1tbl, yo, k1, p2tog, [yo] twice, [p2tog] twice, yo, p8, k to last 2 sts, p2.

Row 7 K2tog, yo, k to marker, ssk, yo, k6, k2tog, yo, k1, yo, p2tog, k1, p1, k3, yo, k1tbl, k1, ssk.

Row 8 P1, kf&b, k1tbl, yo, k1, p2tog, [yo] twice, [p2tog] twice, yo, k3, yo, p2tog, p5, k to last 2 sts, p2.

Row 9 K2tog, yo, k to marker, ssk, yo, k4, k2tog, yo, k5, yo, p2tog, k1, p1, k3, yo, k1tbl, k1, ssk.

Row 10 P1, kf&b, k1tbl, yo, k1, p2tog, [yo] twice, [p2tog] twice, yo, k7, yo, p2tog, p3, k to last 2 sts, p2.

Row 11 K2tog, yo, k to marker, ssk, yo, k2, k2tog, yo, k9, yo, k3, p1, k3, yo, k1tbl, k1, ssk.

Row 12 P1, k1, k1tbl, yo, k1, p2tog, [yo] twice, p2tog, p3tog, yo, k11, yo, p2tog, p1, k to last 2 sts, p2.

Row 13 K2tog, yo, k to marker, ssk, yo, k3, yo, ssk, k7, k2tog, yo, k4, p1, p2tog, yo, k2, k2tog.

Row 14 P1, k1, p2tog, yo, [p2tog] twice, [yo] twice, p2tog, k1, yo, p2tog, k5, p2tog tbl, yo, p4, k to last 2 sts, p2.

Row 15 K2tog, yo, k to marker, ssk, yo, k5, yo, ssk, k3, k2tog, yo, k1, p2tog, k1, p1, p2tog, yo, k2, k2tog.

Row 16 P1, k1, p2tog, yo, [p2tog] twice, [yo] twice, p2tog, yo, p2tog, k1, p2tog tbl, yo, p6, k to last 2 sts, p2.

Row 17 K2tog, yo, k to marker, ssk, yo, k7, yo, k3tog, yo, k3, p1, p2tog, yo, k2, k2tog.

Row 18 P1, k1, p2tog, yo, [p2tog]

twice, [yo] twice, p2tog, yo, p2tog, p7, k to last 2 sts, p2.

Row 19 K2tog, yo, k to marker, ssk, yo, k6, k2tog, yo, k3, p1, p2tog, yo, k2, k2tog.

Row 20 P1, k1, p2tog, yo, [p2tog] twice, [yo] twice, p2tog, yo, p2tog, p5, k to last 2 sts, p2.

Row 21 K2tog, yo, k to marker, ssk, yo, k4, k2tog, yo, k3, p1, p2tog, yo, k2, k2tog.

Row 22 P1, k1, p2tog, yo, [p2tog] twice, [yo] twice, p2tog, yo, p2tog, p3, k to last 2 sts, p2.

Row 23 K2tog, yo, k to marker, ssk, yo, k2, k2tog, yo, k3, p1, p2tog, yo, k2, k2tog.

Row 24 P1, kf&b, p2tog, yo, [p2tog] twice, [yo] twice, p2tog, yo, p2tog, p1, k to last 2 sts, p2.

DECREASING SECTION

NOTE On some rows, you will be placing a new marker and removing the old marker. On all other rows, slip marker as you come to it.

Row 1 (RS) K2tog, yo, k to within 1 st of marker, place new marker, k3tog (removing the old marker), yo, k3, yo, k2, p1, k3, yo, k1tbl, k1, ssk.

Row 2 P1, kf&b, k1tbl, yo, k1, p2tog, [yo] twice, [p2tog] twice, yo, p4, k to last 2 sts, p2.

Row 3 K2tog, yo, k to marker, k2tog, yo, k5, yo, p2tog, k1, p1, k3, yo, k1tbl, k1, ssk.

Row 4 P1, kf&b, k1tbl, yo, k1, p2tog, [yo] twice, [p2tog] twice, yo, p6, k to last 2 sts, p2.

Row 5 K2tog, yo, k to within 1 st of marker, place new marker, k3tog (removing the old marker), yo, k7,

yo, p2tog, k1, p1, k3, yo, k1tbl, k1, ssk.

Row 6 P1, kf&b, k1tbl, yo, k1, p2tog, [yo] twice, [p2tog] twice, yo, p8, k to last 2 sts, p2.

Row 7 K2tog, yo, k to marker, k2tog, yo, k6, k2tog, yo, k1, yo, p2tog, k1, p1, k3, yo, k1tbl, k1, ssk.

Row 8 P1, kf&b, k1tbl, yo, k1, p2tog, [yo] twice, [p2tog] twice, yo, k3, yo, p2tog, p5, k to last 2 sts, p2.

Row 9 K2tog, yo, k to within 1 st of marker, place new marker, k3tog (removing the old marker), yo, k4, k2tog, yo, k5, yo, p2tog, k1, p1, k3, yo, k1tbl, k1, ssk.

Row 10 P1, kf&b, k1tbl, yo, k1, p2tog, [yo] twice, [p2tog] twice, yo, k7, yo, p2tog, p3, k to last 2 sts, p2.

Row 11 K2tog, yo, k to marker, k2tog, yo, k2, k2tog, yo, k9, yo, k3, p1, k3, yo, k1tbl, k1, ssk.

Row 12 P1, k1, k1tbl, yo, k1, p2tog, [yo] twice, p2tog, p3tog, yo, k11, yo, p2tog, p1, k to last 2 sts, p2.

Row 13 K2tog, yo, k to within 1 st of marker, place new marker, k3tog (removing the old marker), yo, k3, yo, ssk, k7, k2tog, yo, k4, p1, p2tog, yo, k2, k2tog.

Row 14 P1, k1, p2tog, yo, [p2tog] twice, [yo] twice, p2tog, k1, yo, p2tog, k5, p2tog tbl, yo, p4, k to last 2 sts, p2.

Row 15 K2tog, yo, k to marker, k2tog, yo, k5, yo, ssk, k3, k2tog, yo, k1, p2tog, k1, p1, p2tog, yo, k2, k2tog.

Row 16 P1, k1, p2tog, yo, [p2tog] twice, [yo] twice, p2tog, yo, p2tog, k1, p2tog tbl, yo, p6, k to last 2 sts, p2.

Row 17 K2tog, yo, k to within 1 st

of marker, place new marker, k3tog (removing the old marker), yo, k7, yo, k3tog, yo, k3, p1, p2tog, yo, k2, k2tog.

Row 18 P1, k1, p2tog, yo, [p2tog] twice, [yo] twice, p2tog, yo, p2tog, p7, k to last 2 sts.

Row 19 K2tog, yo, k to marker, k2tog, yo, k6, k2tog, yo, k3, p1, p2tog, yo, k2, k2tog.

Row 20 P1, k1, p2tog, yo, [p2tog] twice, [yo] twice, p2tog, yo, p2tog, p5, k to last 2 sts, p2.

Row 21 K2tog, yo, k to within 1 st of marker, place new marker, k3tog (removing the old marker), yo, k4, k2tog, yo, k3, p1, p2tog, yo, k2, k2tog.

Row 22 P1, k1, p2tog, yo, [p2tog] twice, [yo] twice, p2tog, yo, p2tog, p3, k to last 2 sts, p2.

Row 23 K2tog, yo, k to marker, sl marker, k2tog, yo, k2, k2tog, yo, k3, p1, p2tog, yo, k2, k2tog.

Row 24 P1, kf&b, p2tog, yo, [p2tog] twice, [yo] twice, p2tog, yo, p2tog, p1, k to last 2 sts, p2.

Rep rows 1–24 eight times more—18 sts.

Next row (RS) K10, p1, k7.

Next row Knit. Bind off loosely purlwise.

FINISHING

Block to finished measurements, pinning holes open along top edge. ●

WEST

Sheep and llamas at play

Company Stats

COMPANY STARTED
1999

PROPRIETORS
Leanne Jannusch Hayne
and John Hayne

LOCATION
Montana

YARNS
Seven types of yarn in addition to roving, quilt and felting batts, all made in the United States and Canada

BUSINESS PHILOSOPHY
To maintain a small retail business that works in harmony with our sustainable, family-owned sheep-ranch business.

WEBSITE
beaverslide.com

Founded by descendants of homesteaders who went West in the early twentieth century, Beaverslide Dry Goods is located on the sparsely populated Montana Rocky Mountain Front on three thousand acres. Four hundred sheep, honeybees and a flock of free-range chickens call the ranch home.

Inspired by Leanne's love of knitting, John's passion for ranching and their strong connection to the land and local ranching community, the Haynes started their company to share their rural life through their natural fiber yarns, striving to provide a unique, affordable product that contributes to sustainable American agriculture and small business.

Raising sheep is a financial challenge in today's market, and the Haynes' yarn business is critical to maintaining ranching endeavors. In an effort to remain as local as possible, they process the yarn at a small, family-owned-and-run mill in Alberta, Canada. The yarn undergoes minimal processing on antique equipment dating back to the 1860s and involves environmentally responsible practices, such as using solar-heated water for scouring as well as mild soaps and dyes. The ranch is located near the Canadian/U.S. border, making it a simple day trip to the mill and back.

With Beaverslide's region considered to be in the top 1 percent of prime wildlife habitat in the United States, there come some interesting challenges. Throughout the year, it is not unusual to have grizzly bears, mountain lions, coyotes, eagles and other wildlife as regular visitors. The combination of these predators and the Beaverslide sheep creates problems from time to time, but the situation is fairly manageable with careful monitoring, electric fences and the addition of a new guard llama named Juan.

Though raised under wholesome and humane conditions, the animals of Beaverslide live in a sometimes extreme climate, so their wool is noticeably "loftier" than imported yarn. Yarns are made from the company's flock of long-fiber Australian Delaine merino sheep. The finished products come in an extensive palette of unique, mulespun color blends available both at the Dupuyer Cache general store and online.

With no plans for retirement at this time, the Haynes are hoping to launch a line of their own handpainted and kettle-dyed yarns in the future.

1. The Montana plains
2. Bottle-feeding the lambs
3. Proud family
4. Juan

■ BEAVERSLIDE DRY GOODS

Nutkin Cardi and Hat

■■■■

SIZES

Instructions for cardigan are written for childs size 4. Changes for sizes 6 and 8 are in parentheses. Instructions for hat are for one size.

FINISHED MEASUREMENTS

CARDIGAN
CHEST (buttoned)
28 (31, 34)"/71 (78.5, 86.5)cm
LENGTH
15½ (16½, 17½)"/39.5 (42, 44.5)cm
UPPER ARM
12½ (13½, 14 ½)"/31.5 (34, 37)cm
HAT
HEAD CIRCUMFERENCE
17¼"/44cm
DEPTH 7"/18cm

MATERIALS

■ 3 (4, 4) 4oz/113g hanks (each approx 241yd/220m) of Beaverslide Dry Goods *Worsted* (fine Beaverslide wool/kid mohair) in winter wheat (MC)
■ 1 hank each in juniper heather (A), autumn haze (B) and gilded earth (C)
■ One pair size 7 (4.5mm) needles *or size to obtain gauge*
■ Two size 7 (4.5mm) double-pointed needles (dpns) for I-cords
■ Size G-6 (4mm) crochet hook
■ Stitch holders
■ Stitch marker
■ 5 row markers
■ Bobbins (optional)

For this kid-friendly cropped sweater, Amy Bahrt drew on her signature whimsical animal motifs, use of texture, unusual color combinations and movable parts. Inspired by falling leaves in autumn, she created borders that mimic the texture of the acorn caps, and included wooden buttons to add to the rustic, homespun feeling.

■ One ⅜"/9mm four-hole cream button (for eye)
■ Six ⅝"/16mm wooden buttons
■ Black sewing thread

GAUGE

18 sts and 26 rows to 4"/10cm over St st and chart pats using size 7 (4.5mm) needles.
Take time to check gauge.

NOTE

Use a separate bobbin (or strand) of yarn for each color section.

SEED STITCH

(over an even number of sts)
Row 1 (RS) *K1, p1; rep from * to end.
Row 2 K the purl sts and p the knit sts. Rep row 2 for seed st.

BACK (CARDIGAN)

With A, cast on 66 (72, 78) sts. Work in seed stitch for 8 rows. Change to MC. Cont in St st until

piece measures 15½ (16½, 17½)"/39.5 (42, 44.5)cm from beg, end with a WS row.

SHOULDER AND BACK NECK SHAPING

Next row (RS) Bind off 20 (23, 25) sts, knit until there are 26 (26, 28) sts on RH needle, place these sts on holder for back neck, bind off rem 20 (23, 25) sts.

LEFT FRONT (CARDIGAN)

With A, cast on 36 (38, 42) sts. Work in seed stitch for 8 rows.
Next row (RS) With MC, k 30 (32, 36) sts, with A, work in seed st over last 6 sts (button band).
Next row With A, work in seed st over first 6 sts, with MC, purl to end. Keeping 6 sts at front edge in seed st (with A) and rem sts in St st, work even for 6 (8, 10) rows more.

BEG CHART PAT I

Row 1 (RS) With MC, k 13 (14, 16), work 11 sts of chart, work to end. Cont to foll chart in this way to row 13, end with a RS row. With MC, work even for 7 rows. Beg chart pat I again as foll:
Row 1 (RS) With MC, k 7 (8, 10), work 11 sts of chart, work to end. Cont to foll chart in this way to row 13, end with a RS row. With MC, work even until piece measures 13 (14, 15)"/33 (35.5, 38)cm from beg, end with a WS row.

NECK SHAPING

Next row (RS) With MC, k 30 (32, 36) sts, place last 6 sts on a holder; cut A. With MC, bind off 4 (4, 5) sts at beg of next row, then at same (neck) edge, bind off 2 sts twice, end with a WS row. Dec 1 st from neck edge on next row, then every other row 1 (0, 1) time more. Work even on 20 (23, 25) sts until piece measures same length as back to shoulder, end with a WS row. Bind off. Place markers for 5 buttons on button band, with the first 1"/2.5cm from lower edge, the last 2 (2¼, 2½)"/5 (5.5, 6.5)cm from neck edge and the others evenly spaced between.

RIGHT FRONT (CARDIGAN)

With A, cast on 36 (38, 42) sts. Work in seed stitch for 14 (16, 18) rows. AT THE SAME TIME, work first buttonhole opposite marker as foll:

Buttonhole row (RS) K1, p1, bind off next 2 sts, work to end.

Next row Work across, casting on 2 sts over bound-off sts. When seed st rows are completed, cont as foll:

BEG CHART PAT II

Row 1 (RS) With A, work in seed st across first 6 sts for buttonhole band, pm, beg and end chart for size being made. Cont to foll chart in this way to row 47. AT THE SAME TIME, cont to work buttonholes opposite markers. When chart has been completed, cont to keep 6 sts at front edge in seed st using A and rem sts in St st using MC until piece measures 13 (14, 15)"/33 (35.5, 38)cm from beg, end with a WS row.

NECK SHAPING

Next row (RS) Work in seed st across first 6 sts, place these sts on a holder; *do not* cut A. With MC, bind off next 4 (4, 5) sts, work to end. At same (neck) edge, bind off 2 sts twice, end with a WS row. Dec 1 st from neck edge on next row, then every other row 1 (0, 1) time more. Work even on 20 (23, 25) sts until piece measures same length as back to shoulder, end with a WS row. Bind off.

SLEEVES (CARDIGAN)

With A, cast on 36 (38, 38) sts. Work in seed stitch for 8 rows. Change to MC. Cont in St st and work even for 6 (6, 2) rows, end with a WS row.

Inc row (RS) K1, M1, k to last st, M1, k1. Rep inc row every 6th row 10 (11, 13) times more—58 (62, 66) sts. Work even until piece measures 12½ (13½, 14½)"/31.5 (34.5, 37)cm from beg, end with a WS row. Bind off.

FINISHING (CARDIGAN)

Block pieces to measurements. Sew shoulder seams.

NECKBAND

With RS facing, place 6 sts on right front neck holder on RH needle. With attached A, pick up and k 19 (19, 20) sts along right neck edge, k 26 (26, 28) sts from back neck holder, pick up and k 19 (19, 20) sts

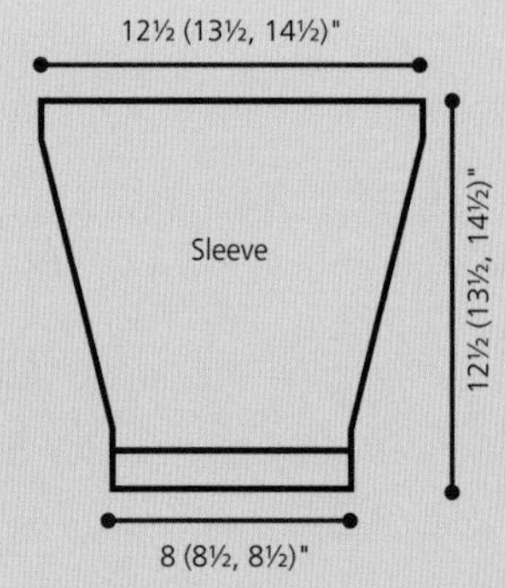
12½ (13½, 14½)"
Sleeve
12½ (13½, 14½)"
8 (8½, 8½)"

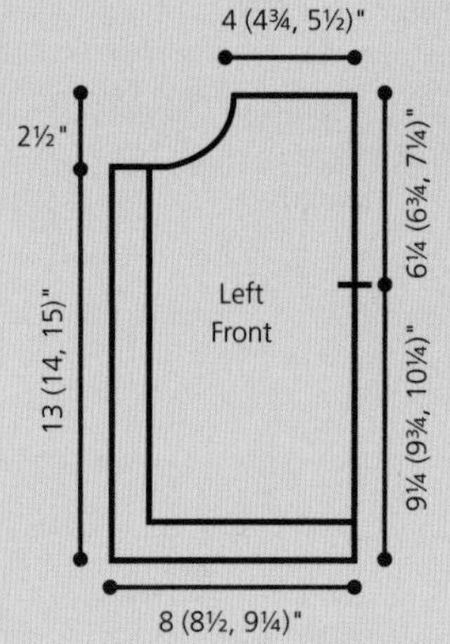
4 (4¾, 5½)"
2½"
Left Front
13 (14, 15)"
6¼ (6¾, 7¼)"
9¼ (9¾, 10¼)"
8 (8½, 9¼)"

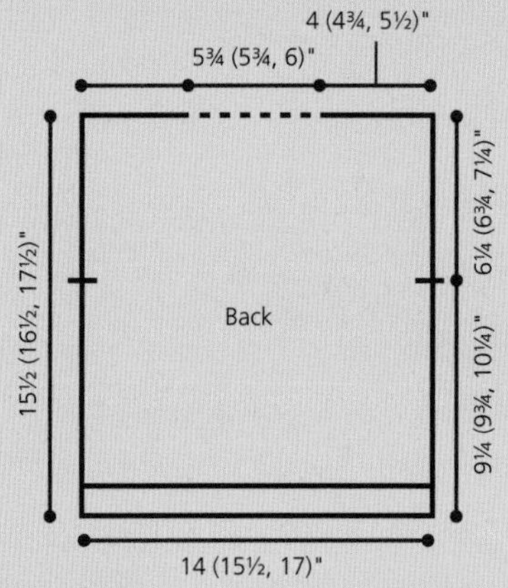
4 (4¾, 5½)"
5¾ (5¾, 6)"
Back
15½ (16½, 17½)"
6¼ (6¾, 7¼)"
9¼ (9¾, 10¼)"
14 (15½, 17)"

Chart I

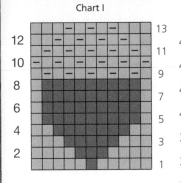

11 sts

Stitch and Color Key

☐ k on RS, p on WS

⊟ p on RS, k on WS

◉ nose placement

⬤ eye placement

🙾 ear placement

☒ gilded earth (C) fringe
placement

🅅 autumn haze (B) fringe
placement

▨ winter wheat (MC)

▨ juniper (A)

▨ autumn haze (B)

Chart II

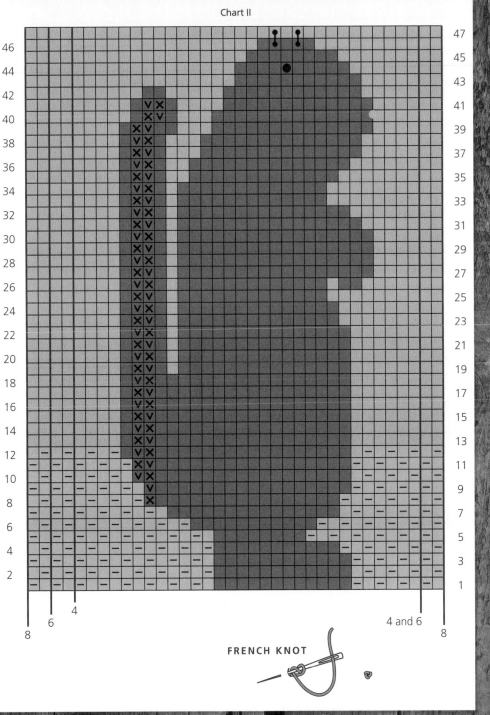

FRENCH KNOT

along left neck edge, work in seed st over 6 sts on left front neck holder—76 (76, 80) sts. Cont in seed st on all sts for 2 rows, end with a RS row.
Buttonhole row (WS) Work to last 4 sts, bind off next 2 sts, work to end.
Next row Work in seed st, casting on 2 sts over bound-off sts.
Work 2 rows more. Bind off in seed st. Place markers 6¼ (6¾, 7¼)"/16 (17, 18.5)cm down from shoulders on back and fronts. Sew sleeves to armholes between markers. Sew side and sleeve seams.

EYE
Using black thread, sew on button eye where indicated on chart, using cross stitches as shown in photo.

NOSE
Using A, embroider a French knot nose (see page 169) where indicated on chart.

EARS (MAKE 2)
With crochet hook and B, ch 7.

Fasten off, leaving a long strand for sewing. Fold chain in half so bottom lps are tog, then whipstitch lps tog to secure. Sew on ears where indicated on chart.

FURRY TAIL
Cut thirty-four 4"/10cm-long strands each of B and C. With crochet hook, attach fringe horizontally as indicated on chart and alternate colors as shown. Trim each fringe to 1"/2.5cm from knot.

ACORN STEMS (MAKE 2)
With dpn and A, cast on 3 sts. Work in I-cord as foll:
Next row (RS) With 2nd dpn, k3, do not turn. Slide sts back to beg of needle to work next row from RS; rep from * 4 times more. Cut yarn, leaving an 8"/20.5cm tail. Thread tail in tapestry needle, then thread through rem sts. Pull tog tightly and secure end, then insert needle down through center of I-cord. Use tail to sew stem to center top of acorn. Sew on wooden buttons.

HAT
With A, cast on 84 sts. Work in seed stitch for 8 rows; cut A leaving a long tail for sewing. Change to MC. Cont in St st and work for 2 rows.

BEG CHART PAT I
Row 1 (RS) With MC, k8, *work 11 sts of chart, with MC, k8; rep from * 3 times more.
Row 2 With MC, p8, *work 11 sts of chart, with MC, p8; rep from * 3 times more. Cont to foll chart in this way to row 13. With MC only, work

even until piece measures 4¾"/12cm from beg, end with a WS row.

CROWN SHAPING
Dec row 1 (RS) *K10, k2tog; rep from * to end—77 sts.
Purl next row.
Dec row 2 (RS) *K9, k2tog; rep from * to end—70 sts.
Purl next row.
Dec row 3 (RS) *K8, k2tog; rep from * to end—63 sts.
Purl next row.
Dec row 4 (RS) *K7, k2tog; rep from * to end—56 sts.
Purl next row.
Dec row 5 (RS) *K6, k2tog; rep from * to end—49 sts.
Purl next row.
Dec row 6 (RS) *K5, k2tog; rep from * to end—42 sts.
Purl next row.
Dec row 7 (RS) *K4, k2tog; rep from * to end—35 sts.
Purl next row.
Dec row 8 (RS) *K3, k2tog; rep from * to end—28 sts.
Purl next row.
Dec row 9 (RS) [K2tog] 14 times—14 sts.
Cut yarn, leaving an 18"/45.5cm tail. Thread through rem sts. Pull tog tightly and secure end, then sew back seam, changing to A over seed st band.

ACORN STEMS (MAKE 4)
Work as for cardigan and sew to center top of acorns. ●

■ MORE WESTERN COMPANIES

Buy local

BIDE A WEE FARM
Newberg, Oregon
bideaweefarm.com

BIG SKY QUALITY WOOL
Broadus, Montana
bigskyqualitywool.com

BLACKWOLF RANCH
Saint Ignatius, Montana
blackwolfranch.com

BLAKESLEY CREEK FARM
Philomath, Oregon
bellwetherwool.com

CORMO SHEEP & WOOL FARM
Orland, California
cormo.us

FOX HOLLOW FIBER
Eugene, Oregon
oregonwool.com

GENESIS ALPACAS
Marysville, Washington
genesisalpacas.com

GOAT KNOLL FARM
Dallas, Oregon
wvi.com~goatknol

HAND JIVE KNITS
California
handjiveknits.com

LONESOME STONE NATURAL FIBER MILL
Granby, Colorado
lonesomestonefiber.com

OLD MILL FARM
Mendocino, California
oldmillfarm.org

OOMINGMAK MUSK OX CO-OPERATIVE
Anchorage, Alaska
qiviut.com

TAPETES DE LANA
Mora, New Mexico
tapetesdelana.com

THIRTEEN MILE LAMB & WOOL COMPANY
Belgrade, Montana
lambandwool.com

VICTORY RANCH
Mora, New Mexico
victoryranch.com

THE DESIGNERS

AMY BAHRT has her own line of knitwear for children and is the author of *Creature Comforts*. She lives in New York City.

FAITH HALE is a former associate editor at *Vogue Knitting* and *Knit Simple* magazines and co-editor of *Knit.1*. She is currently pursuing a new passion in fine bookbinding and lives in New York City.

KIRSTEN KAPUR is a fashion and textile designer. She lives in New Jersey with her husband and three teenaged children. Read her blog at throughtheloops.typepad.com.

ELSPETH KURSH lives in Virginia. A museum specialist and graduate student, she blogs at wrypunster.typepad.com.

A designer from western Massachusetts, **MELISSA LaBARRE** co-wrote *New England Knits*. She blogs at knittingschooldropout.com.

SUSAN LAWRENCE designs knitwear inspired by the beauty surrounding her home in Salt Lake City, Utah. Follow her work at knittingasfastasican.com.

AMY POLCYN has a professional designer since 2005. She lives in Detroit with her husband, daughter and two wool-loving cats. Her website is amypolcyn.com.

KRISTEN RENGREN is the author of *Vintage Baby Knits*. You can read about her at retroknit.net/blog. She lives in Illinois.

Cartographer by day, knitter by night, **ELLI STUBENRAUCH** resides in Waco, Texas. You can find her blog at elliphantom.com.

■ EVENTS AND FESTIVALS

ALASKA FIBER FESTIVAL
Alaska (March)
alaskafiberfestival.org

ALPACAPALOOZA
Washington (April)
alpacawa.org

ANNUAL FINGER LAKES FIBER ARTS FESTIVAL
New York (September)

BAZAAR BIZARRE
Massachusetts (December)
bazaarbizarre.org

BAZAAR BIZARRE
California (November)
bazaarbizarre.org

BEST OF SOUTHWEST FIBER ARTS FESTIVAL
New Mexico (November)

BLACK SHEEP GATHERING
Oregon (June)
blacksheepgathering.org

BUST HOLIDAY CRAFTACULAR
California, New York (December)

CALIFORNIA WOOL & FIBER FESTIVAL
California (September)
fiberfestival.com

CLEVELAND KNIT OUT
Ohio (October)
clevelandknitout.com

COMMON GROUND COUNTRY FAIR
Maine (September)
mofga.org/thefair/tabid/135/Default.aspx

DFW FIBER FEST
Texas (April)
dfwfiberfest.org

ESTES PARK WOOL WORKSHOPS & MARKET
Colorado (June)
estesnet.com/events/woolmarket.htm

FALL FIBER FESTIVAL OF VIRGINIA
Virginia (October)
fallfiberfestival.org

FIBER ARTS FESTIVAL AT BONANZAVILLE
North Dakota (July)
fiberartsfest.com

FIBER COLLEGE
Maine (September)
fibercollege.org

FIBER FALLOUT RETREAT
New Jersey (September)
northcountryspinners.org/retreat.htm

FIBERFEST
British Columbia, Canada (March)

FIBERFEST EUREKA!
Montana (July/August)
fiberfesteureka.org

FIBER IN THE PARK
Illinois (September)
fiberinthepark.com

FIBRE WEEK
Alberta, Canada (June)
oldscollege.ca/programs/ContinuingEducation/fibreweek

FRANKLIN CO FIBER TWIST
Massachusetts (September)
fibertwist.com

GREAT BASIN FIBER ARTS FAIR
Utah (October)
greatbasinfiberartsfair.org

GREATER ST. LOUIS KNITTERS' GUILD KNITTING CAMPS & WORKSHOPS
Missouri (Year-round)
stlouisknittersguild.com/workshops.html

HANDWEAVERS GUILD OF AMERICA
Various locations (June)

HEART OF AMERICA FIBER FESTIVAL
Missouri (June)

HOOSIER HILLS FIBERARTS FESTIVAL
Indiana (June)
hoosierhillsfiberartsfestival.com

INTERKNITS MACHINE KNITTERS GUILD OPEN HOUSE
Illinois (Dates vary)
interknitmk.org

IOWA SUMMER SHEEP & WOOL FESTIVAL
Iowa (June)
iowasheep.com

JAMAICA FIBER FESTIVAL
Vermont (May)
jamaicafiberfestival.org

KNIT & CROCHET SHOW
Various locations (Dates vary)
knitandcrochetshow.com

KNIT OUT/FIBER FEST
British Columbia, Canada (Dates vary)

KNITTERS CONNECTION
Ohio (June)
knittersconnection.com

KNITTER'S DAY OUT
Pennsylvania (September)
knittersdayout.org

A KNITTER'S FANTASY
Ohio (Dates vary)
northcoastknitting.org/akf%20main.htm

KNITTER'S FROLIC
Ontario, Canada (April)
downtownknitcollective.ca/dkc_frolic.html

KNOX FARM FIBER FESTIVAL
New York (September)
knoxfarmfiber.com

LAMBTOWN FESTIVAL
California (July)
lambtown.com

LOUISIANA FIBER ARTS FOR-'EM
Louisiana (September)

MADRONA FIBER ARTS RETREAT
Washington (February)
madronafiberarts.com

MAINE FIBER FROLIC
Maine (June)
fiberfrolic.com

MARYLAND SHEEP & WOOL FESTIVAL
Maryland (May)
sheepandwool.org

MASSACHUSETTS SHEEP & WOOLCRAFT FESTIVAL
Massachusetts (May)
masheepwool.org

MEG SWANSON'S KNITTING CAMPS & RETREATS
Wisconsin (Summer)
schoolhousepress.com/camp.htm

MICHIGAN INTERNATIONAL ALPACA FEST
Michigan (September)
alpacafest.org

MIDWEST FIBER & FOLK ART FAIR
Illinois (July)
fiberandfolk.com

MINNESOTA ALPACA EXPO
Minnesota (April)
minnesotaalpacaexpo.com

MONTANA ASSOCIATION OF WEAVERS & SPINNERS
Montana (Dates vary)
mawsonline.org

MT. BRUCE SHEEP & WOOL FESTIVAL
Michigan (September)
sheepstuff.com/ Festival.html

NATIONAL ALPACA FARM DAY
California (September)

NEW ENGLAND WEAVERS SEMINAR
Massachusetts (July)
newenglandweavers seminar.com

NEW HAMPSHIRE SHEEP & WOOL FESTIVAL
New Hampshire (May)
nhswga.com

NEW YORK STATE SHEEP & WOOL FESTIVAL
New York (October)
sheepandwool.com

NORDIC KNITTING CONFERENCE
Washington (Dates vary)
nordicmuseum.org

NORTHERN MICHIGAN LAMB & WOOL FESTIVAL
Michigan (September)
lambandwoolfestival.com

OREGON FLOCK & FIBER FESTIVAL
Oregon (September)
flockandfiberfestival.com

PENNSYLVANIA ENDLESS MOUNTAINS FIBER FESTIVAL
Pennsylvania (September)
pafiberfestival.com

PITTSBURGH KNIT & CROCHET FESTIVAL
Pennsylvania (February)
pghknitandcrochet.com

SHEEP & FIBER FESTIVAL
New Jersey (September/October)
sheepandfiber.com

SHENANDOAH VALLEY FIBER FESTIVAL
Virginia (October)
shenandoahvalleyfiber festival.com

SHEPHERD'S HARVEST SHEEP & WOOL FESTIVAL
Minnesota (May)
shepherdsharvest festival.org

SNAKE RIVER FIBER FAIR
Idaho (May)
srfiberarts.org

SOCK WARS
Worldwide (May)
sockwars.com

SOUTHEASTERN ANIMAL FIBER FAIR
North Carolina (October)
saffsite.org

SOUTHERN ADIRONDACK FIBER FESTIVAL
New York (October)
washingtoncountyfair.com/ fiber-festival.asp

SOUTH INDIANA FIBERARTS FESTIVAL
Indiana (October)
southernindiana fiberarts.com

STEPHENSEN COUNTY FIBER ART FAIR
Illinois (April)
suzybeggin.com/faf.htm

STITCHES EAST
Maryland (October/November)
knittinguniverse.com/ stitches/east

STITCHES MIDWEST
Illinois (August)
knittinguniverse.com/ stitches

STITCHES WEST
California (February)
knittinguniverse.com/ stitches/west

STITCH 'N PITCH
Various locations (Baseball season)
stitchnpitch.com

SUN VALLEY CENTER ARTS & CRAFTS FESTIVAL
Idaho (August)
sunvalleycenter.org/events/ arts-a-crafts-festival.html

TENNESSEE FIBER FESTIVAL
Tennessee (May)
tnfiberfestival.com

TRAILING OF THE SHEEP FESTIVAL
Idaho (October)
trailingofthesheep.org

VERMONT SHEEP & WOOL FESTIVAL
Vermont (September)
vermontsheep.org/ festival.html

VIRGINIA ANGORA GOAT & MOHAIR
West Virginia (June)
angoragoats.com/ show.html

VOGUE KNITTING LIVE
Various locations (Dates vary)
vogueknittinglive.com

WAYNESBURGH SHEEP & FIBER FESTIVAL
Pennsylvania (May)
sheepandfiber.com

WISCONSIN SHEEP & WOOL FESTIVAL
Wisconsin (September)
wisconsinsheepand woolfestival.com

WISCONSIN SPIN IN
Wisconsin (October)
wispinin.org

WOOL FESTIVAL AT TAOS
New Mexico (October)
taoswoolfestival.org

A WOOL GATHERING
Ohio (September)
my.voyager.net/~nfisher/

WORLD SHEEP & FIBER FESTIVAL
Missouri (September)
worldsheepfest.com

WORLDWIDE KNIT IN PUBLIC DAY
Various locations (June)
wwkipday.com

Shepherd's Wool
Stonehedge Fiber Mill
Made in Michigan · USA

GROWN IN WYOMING,
SPUN IN NEW ENGLAND.

SHELTER is an artisanal, woolen-spun yarn made from the fiber of Targhee-Columbia sheep grown in the American West. The yarn — spun in the historic mill town of Harrisville...

07.9806

SHELTER
100% AMERICAN WOOL

GAUGE
US 7 (4.5mm) 20 stitches = 4 in
US 8 (5mm) 18 stitches = 4 in
US 9 (5.5mm) 17 stitches = 4 in

Solitu

breed specific, small ba
artisan yarn from shee
the Chesa

KLYN TWEE
brooklyntweed.

RESOURCES

ALPACAS OF WINDSWEPT FARM
P.O. Box 1245
Middletown, MD 21769
windsweptalpacas.com

BEAVERSLIDE DRY GOODS
P.O. Box 153
Dupuyer, MT 59432
beaverslide.com

BIJOU BASON RANCH
P.O. Box 154
Elbert, CO 80106
bijoubasinranch.com

BROOKLYN TWEED
brooklyntweed.net

BROWN SHEEP COMPANY
100662 County Road 16
Mitchell, NE 69357
brownsheep.com

BUFFALO GOLD
P.O. Box 516
Burleson, TX, 76097
buffalogold.net

CESTARI
3581 Churchville Avenue
Churchville, VA 24421
cestariltd.com

CONJOINED CREATIONS
P.O. Box 4110
Cave Creek, AZ 85327
conjoinedcreations.com

DREAM IN COLOR
dreamincoloryarn.com

ELSAWOOL
Bayfield, CO 81122
wool-clothing.com

FARMHOUSE YARNS
farmhouseyarns.com

THE FIBRE COMPANY/ KELBOURNE WOOLENS
915 North 28th Street,
2nd Floor
Philadelphia, PA 19130
kelbournewoolens.com
thefibreco.com

GREEN MOUNTAIN SPINNERY
P.O. Box 568
Putney, VT 05346
spinnery.com

HAZEL KNITS
hazelknits.bigcartel.com

IMPERIAL STOCK RANCH
92462 Hinton Road
Maupin, OR 97037
imperialstockranch.com

JUNIPER MOON FARM
1036 Venable Road
Palmyra, VA, 22963
fiberfarm.com

KNIT ONE, CROCHET TOO
91 Tandberg Trail, Unit 6
Windham, ME 04062
knitonecrochettoo.com

KOLLAGE YARNS
3304 Blue Bell Lane
Birmingham, AL 35242
kollageyarns.com

KRAEMER YARNS
P.O. Box 72
Nazareth, PA 18064
kraemeryarns.com

MOREHOUSE FARM MERINO
141 Milan Hill Road
Red Hook, NY 12571
morehousefarm.com

MOUNTAIN MEADOW WOOL
22 Plains Drive
Buffalo, WY 82834
mountainmeadowwool. com

OZARK HANDSPUN
P.O. Box 1405
Jefferson City, MO 65102
ozarkhandspun.com

PAGEWOOD FARM
pagewoodfarm.com

QUINCE & CO.
quinceandco.com

RED BARN YARN
450 Rosemont Ave
Pasadena, CA 91103
redbarnyarn.com

SOLITUDE WOOL
34923 Snickersville
Turnpike
Round Hill, VA 20141
solitudewool.com

STONEHEDGE FIBER MILL
2246 Pesek Road
East Jordan, MI 49727
stonehedgefibermill.com

SWANS ISLAND YARNS
231 Atlantic Highway
(Route 1)
Northport, ME 04849
swansislandblankets.com

AMERICAN-MADE NOTIONS

NEEDLES
Dyakcraft Needles
dyakcraft.com/index.htm

BRITTANY NEEDLES
brittanyneedles.com

Denise Interchangeable
Needles
knitdenise.com

WINDERS
Strauch Fiber
strauchfiber.com

SILVER NEEDLES
allbrands.com/products/abp03 559.html

BLOCKING TOOLS, SOCK KEEPERS, DARNING EGGS, NOSTEPINNES
Knitting Notions
knittingnotionsonline.com

NEEDLE CASES
Circular Solutions
thecircularsolution.com

PHOTO CREDITS

All photography by Scott Jones, except where noted.

Pages 2–3, 5, 6, 35 and endpapers by Marcus Tullis.

Pages 59–60 by Rose Callahan.

Pages 86, 117–118, 167 and 170 by Paul Amato.

All yarn company photos courtesy of the respective companies, except page 95 (photo of Susan Gibbs) by Adrianne L. Shtop.

Yards: 450

Gauge 6 1/2 stitches per inch
Needle Size 3 US
2.75 mm

Hope

3mm (3US) – 28sts = 10cm/ 4"

Hand wash. Lay flat to dry

■ ABBREVIATIONS

approx	approximately	rep	repeat
beg	begin(ning)	RH	right-hand
CC	contrasting color	rnd(s)	round(s)
ch	chain	RS	right side(s)
cm	centimeter(s)	S2KP	slip 2 stitches together, knit 1, pass 2 slip stitches over knit 1
cn	cable needle		
cont	continu(e)(ing)	SKP	slip 1, knit 1, pass slip stitch over
dec	decreas(e)(ing)		
dpn(s)	double-pointed needle(s)	SK2P	slip 1, knit 2 together, pass slip stitch over the knit 2 together
foll	follow(s)(ing)		
g	gram(s)	sl	slip
inc	increas(e)(ing)	sl st	slip stitch
k	knit	ssk	slip, slip, knit
k2tog	knit 2 stitches together	sssk	slip, slip, slip, knit
LH	left-hand	st(s)	stitch(es)
lp(s)	loop(s)	St st	stockinette stitch
m	meter(s)	tbl	through back loop(s)
M1	make 1 (knit stitch)	tog	together
M1 p-st	make 1 purl stitch	WS	wrong side(s)
MC	main color	wyib	with yarn in back
mm	millimeter(s)	wyif	with yarn in front
oz	ounce(s)	yd	yard(s)
p	purl	yo	yarn over needle
p2tog	purl 2 stitches together	*	repeat directions following * as many times as indicated
pat(s)	pattern(s)		
pm	place marker	[ ]	repeat directions inside brackets as many times as indicated
psso	pass slip stitch(es) over		
rem	remain(s)(ing)		

■ KNITTING NEEDLES

U.S.	Metric
0	2mm
1	2.25mm
2	2.75mm
3	3.25mm
4	3.5mm
5	3.75mm
6	4mm
7	4.5mm
8	5mm
9	5.5mm
10	6mm
10½	6.5mm
11	8mm
13	9mm
15	10mm
17	12.75mm
19	15mm
35	19mm

SKILL LEVELS

◼◻◻◻ **BEGINNER** — Ideal first project.

◼◼◻◻ **EASY** — Basic stitches, minimal shaping and simple finishing.

◼◼◼◻ **INTERMEDIATE** — For knitters with some experience. More intricate stitches, shaping and finishing.

◼◼◼◼ **EXPERIENCED** — For knitters able to work patterns with complicated shaping and finishing.

■ INDEX